BREWER STATE JR.
LIBRARY
TUSCALOOSA CAMP

D0811919

LETTERS OF JOSEPH CONRAD TO MARGUERITE PORADOWSKA

JOSEPH CONRAD IN 1896

LETTERS OF JOSEPH CONRAD TO MARGUERITE PORADOWSKA

1890–1920

TRANSLATED FROM THE FRENCH
AND EDITED WITH AN
INTRODUCTION, NOTES, AND APPENDICES

BY

JOHN A. GEE AND PAUL J. STURM

KENNIKAT PRESS
Port Washington, N. Y./London

LETTERS OF JOSEPH CONRAD

Reissued in 1973 by Kennikat Press in an unabridged and unaltered edition with permission
Library of Congress Catalog Card No.: 72-86272
ISBN 0-8046-1747-3

Manufactured by Taylor Publishing Company Dallas, Texas

To

George T. Keating and James T. Babb

PREFACE

ALL except nine of the letters published here were sold at Sotheby's in London on December 18, 1933, and were among the books and manuscripts forming the Conrad Memorial Library of Mr. George T. Keating when he donated it to Yale University in the winter of 1937–38. The nine, running from April 16, 1900, to September 27, 1910, were purchased at the Anderson Galleries in New York on January 19, 1938 (Sale 4365, lot 136) for Mr. James T. Babb, who presented them to the collection soon after. The entire series, with typed translations, is mounted in two three-quarter morocco volumes in the Rare Book Room of the Yale Library.

The series falls into two unequal parts. The first is composed of ninety-two letters from February, 1890, to the middle of 1895; the second, of eighteen from April, 1900, to the end of 1920. Several of the earlier period, including some from the Congo and one from Australia, are definitely known to have been lost either before or after Mme. Poradowska received them. Moreover, the interval of nearly five years between these parts, which commences shortly before Conrad was to marry and to settle permanently in rural England as a writer of fiction, is only the first of many lengthy ones which surely cannot all be accounted for by the undoubtedly greater infrequency of the correspondence from then on. But the earlier, unsettled years have far more interest, and for them, in spite of our knowledge that certain letters are missing, the series may be regarded as, on the whole, remarkably complete.

With the object of best serving the needs of the English reader and at the same time of affording examples of Conrad's French as he actually wrote it, the body of the volume has been devoted to an annotated English translation, and the original text of five of the more individual letters has been printed in an Appendix without critical emendation. In the translation and notes we have followed Conrad in employing, as a rule, the French rather than the Polish Christian names of his relatives. Other Appendices contain an English translation of three Polish letters of January, 1890, from Conrad to Mme. Poradowska's husband; two incomplete, unsent French letters from her to Conrad; a genealogical table showing her and Conrad's relation to each other; and a tabulation—helpful for purposes of dating—of the different kinds of paper used by him throughout this correspondence.

In translating and editing these letters we have become indebted to many people who have generously responded to our calls for assistance. Mlle. Aniela Zagórska, a relative of both Mme. Poradowska and Conrad, supplied the genealogical table already referred to and numerous other facts of primary importance. Valuable information was provided by Mlle. Alice Gachet, the niece of Mme. Poradowska. Mr. John D. Gordan has placed at our command the results of his extensive and thorough investigation—now being published by the Harvard University Press—of the manuscripts and other records pertaining to Conrad's earlier literary career. M. Henry D. Davray and the Hon. Evan Charteris, K.C., have answered letters of inquiry about different matters; Mr. Carl P. Rollins of the Yale University Press has helped in the preparation of Appendix V and designed the book; Miss Theresa Sibielski and Mr. Carleton Ashley have assisted in various ways; and, among the members of the staff of the Yale Library to whom we are particularly grateful, Mr. Samuel Thorne, Jr., has aided with problems relating to geography, and Mr. Leon Nemoy with ones arising from our ignorance of Polish and concerning, for the most part, the translations in Appendix I. Miss Emily H. Hall and her assistants in the Rare Book Room have shown us many courtesies. Finally, most of the work in preparing the manuscript for the press was done by Mrs. John A. Gee—to her too we owe many thanks.

J. A. G.
P. J. S.

Yale University
January 25, 1940

CONTENTS

ILLUSTRATIONS

The pictures of Conrad and Mrs. Conrad are reproduced from two photographs which, mounted on the same kind and size of paper, are evidently identical with those sent to their friends with the card announcing their marriage. See Jessie Conrad: *C. and His Circle,* pp. 19 f., and Garnett: *Lrs. from C.,* p. 47. The one of Conrad has not heretofore been published; the one of Mrs. Conrad is part of a larger photograph published in *C. and His Circle,* opp. p. 16.

INTRODUCTION

IN "Heart of Darkness," though a reader of that story could hardly suspect it, there is a hint—the only one in his works—of a relationship vital in Joseph Conrad's life during most of the long period he was writing his first novel, *Almayer's Folly.* It will be remembered that Marlow, in his determination to go to Africa, turned to "an aunt, a dear enthusiastic soul." "I," he says, "Charlie Marlow, set the women to work—to get a job." As Marlow was helped to the command of a "two-penny-half-penny river-steamboat" plying the Upper Congo, so Conrad before him had been similarly aided by one whom he called "Aunt." She, not really his aunt at all but the widow of a somewhat distant cousin, was Marguerite Poradowska. Born of French parentage in Brussels, where she spent a great deal of her life, she had influential connections among the rulers of the Belgian colonial empire. Through them she was instrumental in securing for Conrad, when his own efforts and those of others had seemed on the point of failing, the post that took him to the Congo, and he acknowledged gracefully, if rather obliquely, the service which was to result in so much of his future physical and mental suffering, even though it opened to him the terrible phantasmagoric world of "Heart of Darkness."

Their relationship was far more significant than this passing reference and this particular service would indicate; it bridged a crucial time in his life. A lonely stranger in the difficult land of his adoption, Conrad desperately needed the affection of a truly congenial spirit, and there were reasons why Marguerite Poradowska, more than another, might give him—even though the Channel lay between them—something of the human warmth and sympathetic understanding he ever craved with almost abnormal passion. In a modest way she was an author and had published several original works as well as translations and adaptations from the Polish, chiefly in the *Revue des Deux*

Mondes. Probably she was the first published author of fiction whom Conrad had known; and at the time he was beginning *Almayer's Folly,* though with how serious a thought of publication it is hard to say, such a fact would of itself have caused him to regard her with particular interest. But they had also become acquainted under tragic circumstances—at the deathbed of her husband—and to Conrad's impressionable mind this set her in a poignantly romantic light, pathetic, appealing, especially as she was an extraordinarily beautiful woman.

Following an absence of over two years in the East, during which he had met Almayer and obtained his first command, Conrad returned to London about the middle of 1889. And when in January, 1890, he was planning a long-deferred journey to the Ukraine to visit his beloved uncle and guardian, Thadée Bobrowski, he settled on the route through Brussels so that he might call on his maternal grandmother's first cousin, Alexandre Poradowski, then dying in exile. Poradowski, like other Polish patriots of his generation, had had a variety of careers and endured such extremes of misfortune as were entailed in the great military insurrection of 1863. Under the nickname of *Ostroga* ("Spur") he gallantly commanded a company in that stirring but futile uprising, was taken prisoner, and, as an officer in the Russian army, was condemned to death. His escape, however, was effected by a friend, a fellow Russian officer. In exile Poradowski lived in Dresden and Paris, finally moving to Brussels, where he met Marguerite Gachet. The girl's father, Emile Gachet, a native of Lille, had come to Belgium in 1835. He was associated with the royal Belgian archivist, and later became head of the bureau of paleography. A distinguished scholar, he published several editions of Old French texts and undertook to compile a general vocabulary of the literature of the Middle Ages. After his early death in 1857, the work was completed and issued by Liebrecht.

Mme. Gachet, née Jouvenel, was left with two small children, Marguerite and Charles. As Marguerite grew in beauty she was beset by many suitors. Among these was M. Charles Buls, who later became burgomaster of Brussels. She might well, it would appear, have made any match she chose, but it was the romantic Polish exile, by no means a rich man, who won her. Mme. Charles Zagórska, a relative by marriage, described Alexandre Poradowski as irresistible, keenly intelligent, "with a very special charm." And in her old age Mme. Poradowska revealed to Mlle. Aniela Zagórska, who has kindly passed on the information to us, some of the details of this courtship. Marguerite's mother, horrified that her daughter should have fallen in love with a destitute Polish émigré, nevertheless promised him the girl's hand when he should be able to provide for her. The lovers had to separate, and Poradowski went to Galicia, where Mme. Gachet doubtless hoped he would remain. But to her considerable chagrin the Pole returned at the end of a year, having gained possession of a small property in the neighborhood of Lemberg, and we are told that Mme. Gachet was so upset at the reappearance of her future son-in-law that she fainted. For a time the Poradowskis lived in the country, subsequently residing for several years in Lemberg. In 1884 they removed to Brussels because of Marguerite's health. There Alexandre Poradowski helped to found a charitable organization for Polish refugees and became noted for his great generosity to his compatriots. He died at the age of fifty-four on February 7, 1890, after many years of illness.

Following his death, Mme. Poradowska spent some months in Lublin, Poland, with her husband's relatives, who much admired her. After this visit she resided mostly in Brussels, Lille, and Paris, for many years maintaining an apartment at 84 Rue de Passy. Steadfastly declining to remarry, she continued writing into the second decade of this century. As early as 1924 she was, by the testimony of Mlle. Aniela Zagórska, seriously afflicted by the encroachments of age, and before her death in 1937, at eighty-nine, she had fallen into complete senility. The last years of her life were spent with her nephew, M. Jean Gachet de la Fournière, at the Château de Montgoubelin, St. Benin d'Azy, Nièvre.

Of Mme. Poradowska's literary career there is little to say. Her works, which began appearing in the 1880's, are for the most part concerned with Polish life and customs, and such interest as they had was ephemeral. The reader of these letters will see that Conrad professed an ecstatic admiration for all she wrote; and not merely a general approval, but one extending even to minute details. It must be wondered whether Conrad's taste was faulty, or if perhaps he was blinded by the woman's great personal charm and won over by the kindly interest she took in all he did and by the extreme goodness of her heart. His judgment was indeed compounded of many elements. He was painfully averse to hurting the feelings of anyone dear to him; moreover, in her works she treated of people and things so entwined in the memories of his early life that he could hardly judge impartially, let alone condemn, what to him was not so much literature as the re-creation of his past. But most important was the subconscious feeling Conrad must have had that not to approve wholeheartedly of what Mme. Poradowska wrote would be an act of ingratitude all the more unpardonable because in her letters and their occasional meetings she gave him the impression of being a kindred soul, facing problems similar to his, both literary and personal, and thereby satisfied at a peculiarly desolate time that imperious hunger, which was not only Conradian but Slavic, for intimacy and mutual confidence.

Many times in his letters Conrad returned to the theme of his gratefulness, and there can be no doubt that the several years preceding his marriage were lonely ones, during which he was far from the few people dear to him, often ill, living almost literally from hand to mouth, tortured by doubts as to his future, mistrustful of his literary talents, undecided as to how he might eventually earn a living, and torn between his love for the sea and a shrewd realization that it offered him little promise of security. It is not at all unlikely that Marguerite Poradowska, partly through her example and partly through the reassurance her sympathy gave him, impelled him to complete *Almayer's Folly.* "You have given my life," he wrote, "a new interest and a new affection." It is hard to exaggerate the tonic effect of this relationship, by all odds his most intimate between 1890 and 1895; it must surely have been decisive to his future.

The new interest was to detract somewhat from the passionate introspection which often made Conrad sink so far into melancholia that it was only by an extreme exertion of the will that he could force himself to action: "For a long time I have been uninterested in the end to which my road leads. I have gone along it with head lowered, cursing the stones. Now I am interested in another traveler; this makes me forget the petty troubles of my own road." And yet more pertinent: "What touches me is . . . knowing there is someone in the world who takes an interest in me, whose heart is open to me. . . ."

The value of this correspondence derives from several sources. By far the greater part falls in the years 1890–95, a period hitherto almost devoid of Conrad's published letters and obviously important as that of his literary beginnings. These five years left their mark not merely in the writings that grew directly from Conrad's experiences of the time, but on his entire subsequent history. Loneliness and fierce struggle and disease cannot leave unscarred a man of such temperament. His letters to Mme. Poradowska, though by no means of uniform interest, personal or literary, grant a closer approach to that rich and often baffling nature which was Joseph Conrad. We may see the elements of melancholy and sturdy pessimism, of poetry and ironic humor, in the process of crystallizing, as it were, in literary form.

A certain amount has been said, chiefly by M. Jean-Aubry, concerning Conrad's knowledge of the French language. It appears from these letters that some modification is required of the biographer's encomiums. In this book are presented for the first time, except in facsimile, examples of Conrad's French reproduced with every effort towards accuracy. Very few of the letters published in the *Lettres françaises* have been available to us for study in manuscript, but we believe it just to suppose that throughout the volume the editor, while allowing some mistakes to stand, made corrections so numerous as to give an erroneous representation of Conrad's French composition. There is, for example, the matter of accents, a ticklish problem at best. Many Frenchmen tend to omit certain ones in writing rapidly, or else to pepper the page with ambiguous marks which the reader may interpret at his pleasure. But though it may be assumed that most Frenchmen know their own language, it is another thing to take it for granted that a foreigner's recurrent mistakes in this direction, and in others as well, are simply due to carelessness. As the task of separating ignorance from accident is so delicate, we have, in the five letters presented in Appendix II, preferred not to accept it.

Like all Poles of good family, Conrad learned French in his childhood, and it is said that his French accent, unlike his English one, was quite pure. In the years following, which included several in Marseilles, it is unlikely that he had had much occasion to write the language; hence his fairly constant uncertainty in details of grammar, spelling, and vocabulary. Evidence of his solid grounding in French is the fact that he almost never confused genders, a rare accomplishment in a foreigner. He had difficulty, however, in distinguishing between the *-ai* ending of the future and the *-ais* ending of the conditional, often using the latter for both tenses. Many anglicisms, too, rather than polonisms, had crept into his French: frequently he capitalized the names of the months, gave *exemple* the English spelling, and confused *-ance* and *-ence* endings. One of his most characteristic mistakes—not to be found in the *Lettres françaises*—is his habit of writing *présant* for *présent;* and another, more of character than of language, is his usual capitalization of the word *vous*. It may be guessed that this latter was owing more to politeness than to ignorance.

On many occasions Conrad's French shows itself capable of considerable spontaneity and of responding adequately to the flow of his thought. The letters in Appendix II are sufficient to demonstrate the defects and merits of his French style, which even at its best remains curiously personal and un-French. Seldom can the reader wholly escape the feeling that Conrad's manner was constrained by the yoke of language, that he would scarcely have written in Polish or English just what he wrote in French. But these remarks, which would be embarrassingly obvious if no urgent claim had been made for the excellence and polish of Conrad's French, must not cause one to lose sight of its virtues. Good it is, but in no way comparable to his English, though even of his English it may be said that, rather than assimilating the language, he created another out of it.

LIST OF LETTERS

Part I (1890–95)

1890

1891

1892

1893

1894

1895

Part II (1900–20)

1900

1904

1906

1907

1908

1910

1912

1913

1920

KEY TO REFERENCES

The references to Conrad's works are to the Uniform Edition (J. M. Dent & Sons, Ltd., London) and the Concord Edition (Doubleday, Page & Co., Garden City, N.Y.), which have identical pagination. The following abbreviations are employed:

AF = *Almayer's Folly*
"H. of D." = "Heart of Darkness"
PR = *A Personal Record*
Other abbreviations to be noted are:
LF = Joseph Conrad, *Lettres françaises,* ed. G. Jean-Aubry
LL = G. Jean-Aubry, *Joseph Conrad: Life & Letters*
RDM = *Revue des Deux Mondes*

PART I

1890–1895

LETTERS OF CONRAD TO MME. PORADOWSKA

1890–1895

1. London, 4 February 1890.

Despite the conflicting "tomorrow, Friday," the heading is certainly correct. Not only did 4 Feb., 1890, fall on a Tuesday, but in his letter of 31 Jan. to A. Poradowski (App. I, no. 3) C. wrote that he would leave London on either Tuesday or Wednesday. Later, also, C. gives 5 Feb. as the date of his interview in Brussels with the secretary of the Société belge du Haut-Congo (*LF*, p. 29).

Tuesday, 4 Feb., 1890.[1]

My dear Aunt,

Ever so many thanks for your card.[2] I am leaving London tomorrow, Friday, at nine in the morning and should arrive in Brussels at five-thirty in the afternoon. I shall accordingly be with you[3] about six. Believe me, with the keenest gratitude, your very affectionate nephew and very obedient servant,

Conrad Korzeniowski.[4]

2. Warsaw, 11 February 1890.

11 Feb., 1890. Warsaw.

My dear and good Aunt,

I am writing this note to tell you that Charles Zagórski has left Warsaw for Lublin, with the result that I have not yet seen anyone in the family.[1]

1. In a large hand that cannot be identified as C.'s, "Maliszewski" is penciled below the heading. This was probably Edward Maliszewski (1875–1928), a writer on Polish nationalism. See *Ilust. encyk. Trzaski* . . ., III, 311. His "Dictionnaire biographique des personnes qui ont pris part à l'insurrection de 1863" (MS. in the Biblioteka narodowa, oddział Rapperwilski, Warsaw) contains a descriptive account of A. Poradowski's military service in behalf of the Polish cause. (For this information, and for a transcription of this account, we are indebted to Mlle. Aniela Zagórska.)

2. In answer to C.'s letter of 31 Jan. to her husband (App. I, no. 3), who was evidently too ill to reply (see L. 2, n. 2).

3. She resided in the Rue Veydt. (From her husband's obituary in the *Journal de Bruxelles,* 12 Feb., 1890, a source of information hereafter usually referred to as "A. Poradowski.")

4. C.'s full name was Józef Teodor Konrad Nałęcz Korzeniowski (Morf, *Polish Heritage of C.*, p. 14; *LL*, I, 290). By far the commonest of the many different signatures of these letters is "J. Conrad."

---

1. Charles Zagórski was C.'s somewhat older second cousin once removed

I was with you in mind and heart yesterday, sharing your grief[2] though far from you—as indeed I have not ceased doing since I left you. I am departing tomorrow evening and shall have to find Charles before calling upon the Zagórskis. He did not leave his address in Warsaw—at least not with anyone I know.

I called at the offices of the *Słowo,* but without finding the editor in.[3] I left the announcement and my card, and shall drop in again tomorrow.

Au revoir, my dear Aunt. If I know not how to say all I feel, you will think me none the less your affectionate nephew, friend, and very obedient servant,

C. Korzeniowski.

I shall write from Lublin, or from Kazimierówka[4] on arrival.

3. Lipovets, Ukraine, 15 (and 16?) February 1890.

The heading demands some alteration, for 14 Feb., 1890, was a Friday. But 15 Feb., though in every way more probable (see esp. L. 2 and the first paragraph below), was perhaps not the date of the entire letter. According to a memorandum by his uncle as cited by Jean-Aubry, C. arrived at Kazimierówka on 16 Feb. (*LL,* I, 123). And in a passage in *PR* which is without question fundamentally an account of this visit rather than the one in 1893 (see esp. p. 22, ll. 12 f.), C. speaks of arriving at a town on the railroad (i.e., Lipovets), of being met in the evening by his uncle's major-domo, and of starting out the next morning by sledge and reaching Kazimierówka soon after nightfall, a journey usually requiring about eight hours (pp. 20–22). There is, then, though the letter itself contains

and Mme. P.'s nephew by marriage. See App. IV. For C.'s deep affection for him, see *LL,* I, 228 f. Having "turned to growing wheat on paternal acres" (*PR,* p. 19), he lived in Lublin (about 95 mi. SE. of Warsaw) with his parents (Jean and Gabrielle), wife (Angèle), aunt (Jeannette), and two small daughters (Aniela and Karola). See Lrs. 3 and 10, and App. IV.

2. Her husband died on 7 Feb. ("A. Poradowski").

3. The *Słowo* was a conservative daily of which the novelist Henryk Sienkiewicz had been the editor since 1882. See *Annuaire de la presse française . . .* for 1891, p. 715, and *Ilust. encyk. Trzaski . . .*, V, 15. A. Poradowski had been the Brussels correspondent ("A. Poradowski").

4. For the location of this Ukrainian village, see L. 4, n. 1. His Uncle Thadée, whom he was about to visit, lived here.

no substantial indication of any interruption, some reason to suspect that its second part (beginning with "That is all") may have been written Sunday morning, 16 Feb.

Saturday, 14 Feb., '90. At Lipowiec,[1] en route to Kazimierówka.

My dear Aunt Marguerite,

Yesterday I left Lublin without being able to find a free moment to write the letter I promised you. Excuse this delay of twenty-four hours in reporting my sad mission.

All those good souls[2] so tried by grief think constantly of you. They learned the news some hours before my arrival through the obituary in the newspaper, but it must not be disclosed to Aunt Jeannette and poor Uncle Jean, who is, alas, quite ill. And all those unhappy creatures, crushed by the blow befalling them, and living in almost daily expectation of another death[3] in the family, gathered themselves around me, asking, "And Marguerite?" "Poor Marguerite?" Aunt Gabrielle wanted to know everything, and with an aching heart I had to tell the story of your sad ordeal. I described you as I saw you: kind, loving, devoted, and courageous. But they know you so well! Appreciate you so deeply! All of them—Gabrielle, Angèle, and Charles—have hearts of gold. The announcement of your visit to Poland[4] was as a flash of light in the gloom of our meeting. Aunt Gabrielle is expecting you. I told them everything I knew of your plans. They will write you. They await you with open arms.

That is all, dear Aunt. I leave here in ten minutes. My uncle[5] is waiting for me. His servant,[6] who is accompanying me, says the dear old man has hardly slept since re-

1. In the Govt. of Kiev, Ukraine, and about 300 mi. SE. of Lublin.

2. For the Zagórskis and their relation to C. and Mme. P., see L. 2, n. 1, and App. IV.

3. Both Jean Zagórski and his sister-in-law Jeannette died during 1891. See Lrs. 17 and 26.

4. In the fall of 1890. See the next to the last paragraph and n. 12 of L. 10.

5. Thadée (Tadeusz) Bobrowski (1829–94), "the wisest, the firmest, the most indulgent of guardians" (*PR*, p. 31). *AF* was dedicated to his memory. For an account of his life see *Polski słownik biog.*, II, 163 f.; for a brief eulogy by C., *LL*, I, 291.

6. For a few details about him on this occasion, see *PR*, pp. 20 f.

ceiving my telegram of last Tuesday. I shall write to you soon.

Yours with sympathy and affection,

CONRAD KORZENIOWSKI.

Excuse this letter, dear little Aunt. I write you in French because I think of you in French; and these thoughts, so badly expressed, spring from the heart, which knows neither the grammar nor the spelling of studied commiseration. This is my excuse.

I have finished *Yaga*[7]—twice. While still under its spell I say nothing of it. By and by I shall write critically—and soon.

Yours,[8]

J. C. K.

4. KAZIMIERÓWKA, UKRAINE, 10 MARCH 1890.

10 Mar., 1890. Kazimierówka.

My dear Aunt,

It was only yesterday that I received your letter of the 15th of February through our good Aunt Gabrielle. The delay is explained by our absence from Kazimierówka,[1] where we yesterday returned after a tour of ten days in the country hereabout.

Thanks ever so much for your kind remembrance of me. My admiration and friendship deepen with a feeling of keen gratitude for your goodness to me. The thought of again seeing you in Brussels will console me when the moment comes to part from my uncle. I leave him the 15th[2] of April and shall have the pleasure of seeing you the 23d of the same month, if all goes well.

7. A novelette of Ruthenian life by Mme. P., her first and probably best-known work of this kind. It appeared in *RDM* for 1 and 15 Aug., 1887, and in book form (P. Ollendorff, Paris) in 1888.

8. The word is in English.

---

1. A small settlement of some thirty houses lying to the west of Skvira, Govt. of Kiev, in approx. 49° 43′ N. and 29° 33′ E. See the Imperial Russian General Staff map (1:420,000) of European Russia (1888), sheet 31 ("Kiev").

2. C. later decided upon the 18th (L. 6).

I am very happy to know that the Princess[3] has been so exceedingly kind and friendly to you, but I dare hope that you will make no hasty decision.[4] And at all events you will not have to decide until about the end of April. By that time I should be with you and able to give you in person the information relative to the trip to Poland.

I read M. Merzbach's speech[5] with melancholy pleasure. He employed no set phrases but recounted that very simple and noble life in words which, while few, came from the heart; and he recognized—I do not say "appreciated," but "recognized"—the part you played in that life.

I beg your pardon for the shortness of this letter. The post leaves today and I have received a batch of mail requiring immediate answer. I believe that the recommendation in my behalf to the Company of the Congo[6] was not strong enough and that the affair will not go through. That vexes me somewhat.

Au revoir, dear Aunt—but not for long, for the time goes quickly. I kiss your hands and embrace you heartily.

Your affectionate nephew,

C. KORZENIOWSKI.

My address: Mr. T. Bobrowski, Lipowiec post-office, for Kazimierówka, Govt. of Kiev, South Russia (for Conrad).

3. Mlle. Alice Gachet has suggested that the allusion may be to Princess Marguerite Czartoryska (1846–93), but the obituary of A. Poradowski points rather to the Dowager Princess de Ligne (1815–95), who is mentioned as having been his close friend. Born Princess Hedwige Lubomirska, in 1836 she married Prince Eugène de Ligne, whom she survived by fifteen years. She lived at the Château de Belœil near Mons, and during 1894 established a residence in Paris. She died in Brussels. See *Almanach de Gotha* for 1896, pp. 353–355, 404 f., and 1312; for 1895, p. 426.

4. Probably as to her permanent residence. The Princess may have asked Mme. P. to reside with her. For a further indication of her interest in this decision, see L. 20, which also reveals Mme. P.'s difficulty in making up her mind. She eventually decided to keep an apartment in Passy (Lrs. 21 and 24).

5. Extracts from this speech were printed in the obituary of A. Poradowski. Henryk Merzbach (1837–1903) was a Polish poet and journalist living in Brussels after 1863. He was a founder with A. Poradowski of the Société de bienfaisance polonaise, and was its vice-president. A. Poradowski had been its secretary. See "A. Poradowski" and *Ilust. encyk. Trzaski . . .*, III, 453 f.

6. The Société anonyme belge pour le commerce du Haut-Congo. A letter (24 Sept., 1889) recommending C. to A. Thys of this company is in Jean-Aubry, *C. in the Congo,* p. 25. See also *ibid.*, pp. 26–37, and *infra,* App. I, no. 1.

Do not write unless you feel inclined to, for we shall be able to chat a little in a few days.

5. Kazimierówka, 23–25 March 1890.

The postscript is dated 25 Mar.

23 Mar., 1890. Kazimierówka.

My dear Aunt,

I have just received your letter, which I read with much sadness. Life rolls on in bitter floods, like the grim and brutal ocean under a sky covered with dark clouds, and there are days when the poor souls who have embarked on the disheartening voyage imagine that never has a ray of sun been able to break through that dreary veil; that never will the sun shine again; that it has never even existed! Eyes that the sharp wind of grief has filled with tears must be pardoned if they refuse to see the blue; lips that have tasted the bitterness of life must be pardoned if they refuse to utter words of hope. Especially must the unhappy souls be pardoned who have elected to make the pilgrimage on foot, who skirt the shore and gaze uncomprehendingly upon the horror of the struggle, the joy of victory, and the deep despair of the vanquished; those souls who receive the castaway with a smile of pity and a word of prudence or reproach on their lips. They especially must be pardoned, "for they know not what they do!"

This is how I feel about him,[1] about you, about those[2] with you; but I ask you to remember, I beg you to understand, that it is permitted a soul dwelling in a body tortured by pain, exhausted with illness, to have these moments of aberration. Under the stress of physical suffering the mind sees falsely, the heart errs, the soul unguided wanders in an abyss.

Now that soul is delivered; it has recognized its error. It requires your pardon. You must give it, wholly, without reserve, with complete forgetfulness of your personal suffering; not as a sacrifice, but as a duty. So given, your

1. Though it is uncertain who is meant, the context and date suggest her late husband. (See also L. 29, n. 4, and L. 39, n. 1.)

2. Probably her relatives in Brussels.

pardon will incline a little towards the human ideal of Divine Justice, towards that Justice which is the only hope, the only refuge, of souls who have fought, suffered, and fallen in the struggle with life.

And since this letter is on the theme of forgiveness, I ask it also for myself. If this letter causes you disappointment or pain, do not condemn me. Wait. Later you will perhaps see that I have tried to tell you only what I thought the truth; and if I grieve you now, you will pardon me then.

Au revoir, dear and good Aunt. I am ever your very sincere and most devoted servant and friend,

J. C. Korzeniowski.

I asked my uncle his opinion as to your visit to Russia.[3] There will be no difficulty. As an Austrian or French subject,[4] you can return without the least fear.

I hesitate to send you this, but *fiat justitia,*[5] *ruat cœlum.* You will understand me! Yours.
25 Mar.

6. Kazimierówka, 14 April 1890.

14 Apr., 1890. Kazimierówka.

My dear Aunt,

I have received your charming, kind letter; and the proof of friendship you give me in concerning yourself with my African projects touches me more than I can say. Ever so many thanks for your kind pains;[1] I impatiently await the moment when I shall be able to kiss your hands while thanking you in person.

I leave my uncle in four days; I have visits to make en route (among others one of forty-eight hours in Lublin)[2]

3. That is, to Poland, then under Russian rule.

4. Mme. P. was a French subject by birth and an Austrian subject by marriage, her husband having lived in Galicia prior to 1884, when he settled in Brussels ("A. Poradowski").

5. C. has written *justicia.*

---

1. See "H. of D.," pp. 53 and 59, where C. acknowledges these services in more detail.

2. He apparently left Lublin on 22 Apr. See Jean-Aubry, *C. in the Congo,* p. 43.

and so shall not be in Brussels before the 29th[3] of this month. Then we shall discuss your idea of visiting Poland and your plans for the future, which interest me deeply, as you may well believe.

I wonder if you received my last letter? At present I am troubled by doubts. Did I understand you correctly? Did my answer offend you? Please in reading it think of my firm attachment to you and to the memory of my poor, dear Uncle Alexandre. So be lenient, my dear, good Aunt.

Au revoir, then, for a little while. There are visitors and I have just escaped for a moment to write these few words. I am being called!

I kiss your hands. Your very devoted friend and nephew,

J. C. KORZENIOWSKI.

7. TENERIFFE ISLAND, CANARY ISLANDS, 15 MAY 1890.

15 May, 1890. Teneriffe.

My dear little Aunt,

Suppose I tell you at the beginning that I have escaped the fever thus far! If I could only assure you that all my letters would start with this good news! Well, we shall see! Meanwhile I am comparatively happy, which is all one can hope for here on earth. We left Bordeaux on a rainy day.[1] A dreary day, a not very merry sailing: haunting memories; vague regrets; still vaguer hopes. One is sceptical of the future. For indeed, I ask myself, why should anyone have faith in it? And so why be sad? A little illusion, many dreams, a rare flash of happiness; then disillusion, a little anger and much pain, and then the end—peace! That is the program, and we have to see this tragi-comedy through. We must resign ourselves to it.

The screw turns, taking me into the unknown. Happily there is another I who roams over Europe, who is at this

3. To A. Thys, of the Société belge du Haut-Congo, C. wrote on 11 Apr. that he would be in Brussels not later than 30 Apr. (*LF*, pp. 29 f.). Jean-Aubry places his arrival a few days earlier (*LL*, I, 124, and *C. in the Congo*, p. 37).

1. In the S.S. ''Ville de Maceio'' on or about 10 May. See the *Mouvement géographique* for 4 May, 1890, p. 36, and Jean-Aubry, *C. in the Congo*, p. 41, n. 2. Cf. *LL*, I, 125.

moment with you, who will go before you to Poland. Another I who moves from one place to another with great ease, who can even be in two places at once. Don't laugh! I really believe this has occurred; I am quite serious. So don't laugh; however, I permit you to say, "How foolish he is!" This is a concession. Life is made up of concessions and compromises.

Speaking of that, how is the Bishop?[2] Have you compromised with the Bishop? A little with your conscience and a great deal with your heart? And so, have you begun to live? Tell me everything when you write.

I am addressing this letter to your mother, to whom I humbly present my respects, as also to your sister-in-law.[3] A hug for the children.[4] Tell them I send my love.[5]

I kiss your hands and commend myself to your heart.

Your entirely devoted

CONRAD.

My compliments to Mme. and M. Bouillot.[6] I have perhaps misspelled this;[7] I mean those living in the Rue Godecharles.

8. LIBREVILLE, FR. EQUAT. AF., TO BOMA, BELGIAN CONGO, 10–12 JUNE 1890.

See the opening paragraph and L. 9, n. 2.

10 June, 1890. Libreville, Gabon.

Dear little Aunt,

As this is the last port of call before Boma,[1] where my

2. Further references evidently to the same person, whom we cannot precisely identify, appear in App. III, no. 2, and L. 50. He seems to have helped obtain for C. the position now taking him to the Congo.
3. Mme. Charles Gachet, née Maud Chamberlin. (Letter of Mlle. Alice Gachet.)
4. Jean and Alice, the son and daughter of the Charles Gachets (*ibid.*).
5. The last two words are in English.
6. Close friends of Mme. P. in Brussels. See App. III, no. 1. M. Bouillot was a former principal of a lycée (athénée) there ("A. Poradowski").
7. The penultimate letter is hard to decipher, and perhaps C. incorrectly wrote "Bouillet." Cf. the still more incorrect "Bouilhet" in L. 11 (n. 10).

1. Situated on the right bank of the Congo about 60 mi. from its mouth, Boma was in 1890 the administrative capital and principal port of call of the Congo Free State. See the *Congo illustré*, IV, 101–103.

sea-voyage ends, I am beginning this letter here[2] at the moment of departure, having in mind to continue it during the passage and end it the day of my arrival at Boma,[3] where, naturally, I shall post it.

Nothing new as to events. As to feelings, nothing new either. And herein lies the trouble; for if one could get rid of his heart and memory (and also brain), and then get a whole new set of these things, life would become ideally amusing. As this is impossible, life is not so; it is abominably sad! For example, among other things that I shall want to put out of mind, but without hope of success, is the memory of my charming Aunt. Naturally this is impossible; therefore I remember and am sad. Where are you? How are you? Have you forgotten me? Are you being left alone? Are you working? Especially that! Have you found the forgetfulness and peace of creative, absorbing work? So runs my list; I wonder about all these things. You have given my life a new interest and a new affection; I am very grateful to you for this. Grateful for all the sweetness, for all the bitterness, of this priceless gift. I look now down two avenues cut through a thick and chaotic tangle of rank weeds. Where do they lead? You follow one, I the other. They fork. Will you find a gleam of sunlight, however pale, at the end of yours? I hope so! I do wish it for you! For a long time I have been uninterested in the end to which my road leads. I have gone along it with head lowered, cursing the stones. Now I am interested in another traveler; this makes me forget the petty troubles of my own road.

While awaiting the inevitable fever, I am very well.—If my existence is to be at all bearable, I must have letters, many letters. From you, for one. Don't forget what I am telling you, my dear and good little Aunt.

After my departure from Boma[4] there may be a long silence.[5] I shall not be able to write until at Léopoldville.[6] It takes twenty days to go there; afoot too! Horrors!

2. C. was at Libreville (on the Gabon estuary) by 28 May (Jean-Aubry, *C. in the Congo*, p. 45).

3. Probably on 12 June. See L. 9, n. 2. 4. Probably on 13 June. See *ibid.*

5. But, remaining a fortnight or so in Matadi (see L. 9, introd. and nn. 2 and 4), he wrote to her from there on the 18th (i.e., L. 9) and 24th (L. 10, n. 2).

6. On the left bank of the Congo 235 mi. ENE. of its mouth, Léopoldville

Probably you will write to my uncle; such was your intention, I believe. You will be very kind to tell him something of me. For example, that you saw me in Brussels,[7] that I was well in body and mind. This will give him pleasure and make him easier on my account. He loves me dearly, and I grow as sentimental as an old fool when I think of him. Forgive this weakness.

When do you return to Brussels?[8] What are your plans for the future? Tell me of all this in your letters, but don't sit down at your writing-desk until you feel a hearty desire to chat with "the absent one." "The absent one" will be my official title in future. I shall be very happy to know that no one is bothering you, that you are working with a free mind. I await your new work[9] with curiosity and impatience. You will send it to me, won't you?

I have discovered that my Company has an ocean-going vessel and will probably build others. If I could obtain the command of one, it would be much better than the river. Apart from the fact that it is more healthful, one always has the opportunity of returning at least every year to Europe. When you get back to Brussels I should like you to let me know whether any ships are being built, so that I can put in my request. You will be able to learn about this through M. Wauters,[10] while I in the depths of Africa won't have any news. I am sure you will do this for me.

Au revoir, dear Aunt. I love and embrace you.

C. Korzeniowski.

(now the governmental headquarters of the Belgian Congo) officially includes Kinshasa, the port on an inlet of Stanley Pool where C. expected to take command of a steamer of the Upper Congo flotilla. C. arrived at Kinshasa about 2 Aug. (*C. in the Congo*, p. 57). For a picture of the Société belge du Haut-Congo's station there, see the *Congo illustré*, I, 107.

7. For this visit, of which he wrote in L. 6, see "H. of D.," p. 59.

8. She was visiting the Princess mentioned in L. 4. See App. III, no. 1, and L. 10.

9. Her next work to be published was a translation from the Polish. See L. 30, n. 1.

10. A resident of Brussels, A. J. Wauters (b. 1845) was an important figure in the development of the Congo Free State. He was the general secretary of the Compagnies belges du Congo, the founder and editor of the *Mouvement géographique* and the *Congo illustré*, and one of the compilers of the *Bibliographie du Congo, 1880–95*. See the *Congo illustré*, IV, 196, n. 1.

9. Matadi, Belgian Congo, 18 June 1890.

Because C. here mentions having received a letter in Boma "the day before yesterday," the date of the heading appears inconsistent with the first entry in "The Congo Diary": "Arrived at Matadi on the 13th of June, 1890" (p. 161). But it would be a mistake seriously to question either the heading or the entry in the light of these words in the body of the letter, for C. was evidently given to using them loosely. See L. 35, n. 1.

Matadi.[1] 18.6.90.

Thank you! Thanks ever so much, dear Aunt, for your kind and charming letter, which came to meet me at Boma.[2] I have only one beloved little Aunt to think up such pretty surprises. Did it please me?! I have a good mind to say No to punish you for having asked, for having appeared to doubt it!

I leave tomorrow[3] on foot. No donkey here except your very humble servant. A twenty-day caravan.[4] Temperature very bearable here and health quite good. I will write[5] as soon as possible. Just now I embrace you heartily and kiss your hand for having written the words which made me so happy the day before yesterday.[6] Your very loving nephew and devoted servant,

Conrad.

1. A town on the left bank about 35 mi. above Boma, and the farthest navigable point on the Lower Congo below the 200 mi. of rapids. See the *Congo illustré,* I, 20 f., II, 45, 140 f., and the description of Marlow's sojourn there in "H. of D.," pp. 63–70.

2. If, as "The Congo Diary" states (p. 161), C. arrived at Matadi on 13 June, he probably arrived at Boma on 12 June. The first draft of "H. of D." (MS. in the Yale Library) clearly points to the conclusion that he spent only one night in Boma. On p. 41 of this draft is written, "I had one dinner in the hotel"; and on p. 43 the words, "As soon as I could I left for a place thirty miles higher up [i.e., Matadi]," which remain substantially the same in the final version (p. 62), have been written over the words, "I left early next day, etc." Jean-Aubry, also, writes that C. arrived at Boma on the evening of 12 June (*C. in the Congo,* p. 44, n. 2).

3. But see the next note.

4. The entry in "The Congo Diary" for 28 June reads, in part: "Left Matadi with . . . a caravan of 31 men" (p. 162). Having spent about a fortnight at Manyanga (p. 167), C. arrived at Nselemba, by Stanley Pool, on 1 Aug. (pp. 170 f.), the complete journey totaling well over 200 mi. (see p. 162, n. 5). Note the similar journey in "H. of D.," pp. 70–72.

5. He did so on 24 June (L. 10, n. 2).

6. See *supra,* introd. and n. 2.

10. Kinshasa, Belgian Congo, 26 September 1890.

26 Sept., 1890. Kinchassa.[1]

Dearest and best of Aunts![2]

I received your three letters all at once on my return from Stanley Falls, where I went as supernumerary in the vessel "Roi des Belges" to learn the river.[3] I read with joy of your success at the Academy,[4] of which, however, I never doubted. I cannot find words strong enough to make you realize the pleasure your charming (and especially kind) letters have given me. They were as a beam of sunlight piercing the grey clouds of a dreary winter's day. For my days here are dreary. Make no mistake about that! I am truly sorry to have come here. Indeed, I regret it bitterly. With a man's egoism I am going to talk about myself. I cannot escape it. To whom shall I unburden my heart if not to you?! I am certain, in talking to you, of being understood *à demi-mot*. Your heart will guess my thoughts more quickly than I can utter them.

Everything is repellent to me here.[5] Men and things, but especially men. And I am repellent to them, too. From the manager in Africa—who has taken the trouble of telling

1. The home-port of the Upper Congo flotilla. See L. 8, n. 6.

2. A note penciled above by Mme. P. reads, "several letters of the Congo lost." One was written at Matadi on 24 June ("The Congo Diary," pp. 161 f.). See also the end of the present letter.

3. The "Roi des Belges," with C. and Camille Delcommune aboard, left Kinshasa about 4 Aug. and arrived in the region of Stanley Falls, a voyage of about a thousand miles, on 1 Sept. On the 6th C. was placed in temporary command. Leaving either then or soon after, he returned to Kinshasa on the 24th. See Jean-Aubry, *C. in the Congo*, pp. 62–67, where a full account of this voyage will be found. Note the similar voyage in "H. of D.," pp. 92–150. Pictures of the "Roi des Belges" are in the *Mouvement géographique* for 15 Nov., 1891, p. 113, and the *Congo illustré*, III, 21.

4. Her *Demoiselle Micia* (a novelette published in *RDM* for 1 and 15 Dec., 1888, and 1 Jan., 1889, and in book form by Hachette in 1889 and several times thereafter) was one of six works receiving French Academy prizes of 500 frs. The announcement appeared in *Le Temps* for 31 May, 1890. (See also App. III, no. 1.)

5. For further details of this antipathy, see "The Congo Diary," pp. 161 f.; *LL*, I, 325; and "H. of D.," pp. 75 f. *et passim*. Note also "Geography and Some Explorers," p. 17: ". . . the vilest scramble for loot that ever disfigured the history of human conscience and geographical exploration."

a good many people that I displease him intensely—down to the lowest mechanic, all have a gift for getting on my nerves; and consequently I am perhaps not as pleasant to them as I might be. The manager is a common ivory-dealer with sordid instincts who considers himself a merchant though he is only a kind of African shopkeeper. His name is Delcommune.[6] He hates the English, and I am of course regarded as an Englishman here. I can hope for neither promotion nor increase of salary while he remains here. Moreover, he has said that he is but little bound here by promises made in Europe, so long as they are not in the contract. Those made me by M. Wauters[7] are not. Likewise I can look forward to nothing, as I have no vessel to command.[8] The new boat will be finished in June of next year, perhaps.[9] In the meanwhile my status here is vague, and I have been having troubles because of this. So there you are!

As a crowning joy, my health is far from good. *Keep the secret for me,* but the truth is that in going up the river I had the fever four times in two months,[10] and then at the Falls (its native country) I had an attack of dysentery

6. See the *Congo illustré,* II, 33, for his picture and a eulogistic outline of his life. Born in 1859, Camille Delcommune first went to the Congo in the '80's. In Mar., 1890, he returned there as assistant manager of the Société belge du Haut-Congo. At the time of his death at Kinshasa in Dec., 1892, he was manager. Jean-Aubry provides a full account of C.'s relations with him (*C. in the Congo,* pp. 58 ff.), including Marlow's description of him at their first meeting ("H. of D.," pp. 73–75).

7. See L. 8, n. 10.

8. The original intention had been for C. to command the "Florida," but she had gone aground shortly before his first arrival at Kinshasa (*C. in the Congo,* p. 58). Upon his return from Stanley Falls he evidently still expected to command her. She was being fitted out for an expedition of several months up the Kasai, and on 24 Sept. he wrote that he was busy preparing to go on this expedition in a few days (*ibid.,* p. 69). At the end of the present letter, however, he writes that he is leaving at once for Bamou and will be gone two or three weeks. Apparently it was in the interval between the two letters, then, that C. was informed he was not to have this command, which was given to a man named Carlier (*LL,* I, 140, n. 1).

9. In 1891 the "Archiduchesse Stéphanie" and "Princesse Clémentine" were launched (*Congo illustré,* II, 35).

10. That is, evidently, from the time he left Matadi. But note that in "H. of D." the similar voyage up the river lasted two months (p. 92). See *C. in the Congo,* p. 62, n. 1.

lasting five days. I feel rather weak physically and a little bit demoralized, and upon my word I think I am homesick for the sea and long to look again on the plains of that salt-water which has so often cradled me, which has so many times smiled at me under the glittering sunshine of a beautiful day, which many times too has flung the threat of death in my face with a whirl of white foam whipped by the wind under a dark December sky. I regret having to miss all that. But what I regret most of all is having bound myself for three years. True, it is hardly likely I shall serve them out. Either those in authority will pick a German quarrel with me to ship me home (and on my soul I sometimes wish they would), or another attack of dysentery will send me back to Europe, if not into the other world, which last would be a final solution to all my troubles!

For four whole pages I have been talking about myself! I have said nothing of the delight with which I read your descriptions of men and things at home. Truly, while reading your dear letters I forgot Africa, the Congo, the black savages and white slaves (of whom I am one) who inhabit it. I was happy for an hour. Know that it is not a small thing (or an easy thing) to make a human being happy for a *whole* hour. You may well be proud of having done it. And so my heart goes out to you in a burst of gratitude and sincerest, deepest affection. When shall we meet again? Alas, meeting leads to parting; and the more often one meets, the more painful become the separations. Fatality.

While seeking a practical remedy for the disagreeable situation into which I have got myself, I have thought of a little plan—still pretty much up in the air—with which you might perhaps help me. It seems that this Company or another affiliated with it is going to have some ocean-going vessels, and even has one already.[11] Probably that big (or fat?) banker who rules the roost at home will have a sizeable interest in the other Company. If my name could be submitted for the command of one of their ships (whose

11. At the beginning of 1892 no ship of Belgian registry had as yet plied between Europe and the Congo (*Congo illustré*, I, 2).

home-port will be Antwerp), I might on each voyage run off to Brussels for a day or two when you are there. That would be ideal! If they decided to call me home to take a command, I should of course bear the expense of my return passage. This is perhaps not a very practical idea, but if you return to Brussels during the winter you might find out through M. Wauters what is going on, mightn't you, dear little Aunt?[12]

I am sending this in care of the Princess (whom I love because she loves you). Soon you will probably see poor, dear Aunt Gaba[13] and those dear, excellent Charles Zagórskis and their charming little daughters.[14] I envy you! Tell them all that I love them tenderly and that I ask a little in return. Mlle. Marysieńka[15] has probably forgotten the promise she made me of her photograph. I am ever her very devoted cousin and servant. I dare not say "admirer" for fear of my Aunt Ołdakowska,[16] to whom I wish to be affectionately remembered. I urge you by all the gods to keep the secret of my health from *everybody;* otherwise my uncle is sure to hear of it.

I must close. I leave in an hour by canoe for Bamou,[17] to select wood and have it cut to build the station here. I shall remain encamped in the forest two or three weeks,[18] unless ill. I rather like that. Doubtless I can have a shot or two at buffalo or elephant. A hearty embrace. I shall write a long letter[19] by the next post.

Your affectionate nephew,

J. C. K.

12. Mme. P. received this letter in Lublin about 29 Nov., the date that she wrote to A. Thys in Brussels, quoting or paraphrasing parts of it (*LL,* I, 139 f.).

13. That is, Gabrielle Zagórska. See L. 3 and App. IV.

14. Aniela and Karola (App. IV).

15. Mme. P.'s niece by marriage, Marie Ołdakowska. See *ibid.*

16. Mme. P.'s sister-in-law. See *ibid.* (C. appears to have written "Oldaknoska.")

17. In the French Congo, about 30 mi. west of Kinshasa and between two branches of the Djoué River. See *Carte internationale du monde au 1,000,000ᵉ,* "Léopoldville" (S.B. 33), dressé et publié par le Service géographique du ministère des Colonies de Belgique (Feb., 1924).

18. C. had returned to Kinshasa by 19 Oct. (*C. in the Congo,* p. 72).

19. Probably written and lost. See *supra,* p. 15, n. 2.

11. London, 1 February 1891.

Though "February 91" has been written by Mme. P. under the heading, this addition must in itself be regarded as perhaps incorrect. But the collection contains an incomplete, unsent letter of hers (App. III, no. 2) which was evidently a fairly prompt reply to this one. Its date is 4 Feb., 1891, and the preceding Sunday fell on 1 Feb.

London. Sunday.

My dear Aunt,

On my safe arrival here[1] I hastily ran to the doctor,[2] who to commence with put me to bed—on account of my legs. He entirely reassured me as to the general state of my health. I am a bit anemic but organically sound.

I got up today expressly to write. I have just finished a letter to my uncle; I feel much stronger and I don't doubt that in a few weeks I shall be completely restored.

I am ashamed to confess it to your sister-in-law, but I have lost the address she gave me for the package entrusted to me.[3] I hope she will be kind enough to forgive me and will send along the necessary address.

Nothing interesting to tell you. The older I get, the more stupid I become. I could not even invent any news. I am not very cheerful, cooped up as I am. I have books, but books are stupid too. I think I shall be able to go back to work in six weeks. Provided I find any!?

If you think something might be gained by approaching Pécher,[4] I hereby inform you that I am thirty-two years old.[5] Have English Master's Certificate[6] of service in sail

1. During the latter part of January. See *LL,* I, 141.
2. Dr. Ludwig (*LL,* I, 145).
3. C. spent two days in Brussels on his return from the Congo (App. III, no. 2).
4. C. here, and usually elsewhere, incorrectly writes "Pêchet." See App. III, no. 2. Ed. Pécher et Cie, Antwerp, were agents for the "Prince" Steam Shipping Co., Ltd., which, under the control of James Knott of Newcastle-on-Tyne, operated a fleet of vessels of small tonnage mostly in the African service. See the many advertisements in the *Mouvement géographique;* also *Lloyd's Register of British and Foreign Shipping* for 1 July, 1894, to 30 June, 1895, pp. xxiv and lxxi, and, under "Ship Owners and Managers," p. 106. Mme. P. was friendly in Brussels with relatives of the head of the firm (App. III, no. 2).
5. Actually thirty-three. C. was born 3 Dec., 1857 (*LL,* I, 4, n. 2).
6. Dated 11 Nov., 1886. See the photograph in Keating, *C. Mem. Lib.,* opp. p. 230.

and steam. Commanded both,[7] but principally sail. Can furnish good references from owners and also from London merchants. Along with all these assets, I burn with a desire to have the honor of commanding one of M. Pécher's steamers. You may say too that judging from the appearance of my nose I get drunk only once a year, that I seem not to have a leaning towards piracy, and that, from what you know of me, you do not think me capable of embezzlement. I have never been haled into police court and I am able to cast a discreet eye on a pretty face without touching. It is true that I limp, but I am in good company. Timoleon[8] was lame and there is even a devil in the same state, according to what I have heard.

If, after learning all this, he refuses to entrust me with a ship, well, we shall have to abandon him to his sad fate—and look elsewhere.—My respects to your mother and to the younger Mme. Gachet. A hug for the children.[9]

I kiss both your hands and, while waiting to hear from you, am ever—and forever—your very devoted nephew and humble servant,

K. N. Korzeniowski.

My compliments to Mme. and M. Bouillot.[10]

Address: Care of Barr, Moering & Co.,[11] 36 Camomile Street, London, E.C.

7. The bark "Otago" in 1888 and 1889 (*LL*, I, 102–116), and the steamer "Roi des Belges" in 1890 (L. 10, n. 3).

8. Greek statesman and general, and the liberator of Syracuse (*c.* 411–337 B.C.). Plutarch and others, however, say nothing of his having been lame, and C. is probably thinking of Tamerlane, the Oriental conqueror (1336–1405).

9. Jean and Alice Gachet.

10. Misspelled "Bouilhet."

11. Where C.'s friend, Adolf P. Krieger, was employed (*LL*, I, 76). C. was later to be employed by this firm (Lrs. 28 ff.), in which he had a small financial interest (*LL*, I, 91).

12. London, 8 February 1891.

(As with L. 11, "February 91" has been added in Mme. P.'s hand.) Not yet received by Mme. P. when she wrote her unsent answer to L. 11 on 4 Feb. (L. 11, introd.), and revealing C.'s substantial physical improvement since L. 11 was written, the present letter cannot belong to the same Sunday (1 Feb.) that L. 11 does. And, following L. 11 by at least a week, it must also precede L. 13 (dated 17 Feb.) by at least several days. With Sunday, 15 Feb., out of the question, we arrive at 8 Feb.

Sunday evening. London.

My dear Aunt,

Your postcard was mislaid at the office, so I received it only today. I am very sorry to learn you are ill. I am sure you caught cold the evening you saw me off.[1] It was so good to chat with you a few moments more that I didn't protest as I should have done, egoist that I am!

I cannot express my gratitude for your kindness. Ill as you are, you think of me! What touches me is not merely the fact that you wish to be of service to me. It is above all knowing there is someone in the world who takes an interest in me, whose heart is open to me, that makes me happy. Take care of yourself, my dear Aunt, and be especially careful not to go out too soon, before you are quite well.

As for me, I am better; I feel stronger and more inclined to live—or, at least, to endure existence. The said existence is rather monotonous at present. I go out little, in order not to tire my legs. It may be that I shall go to Antwerp next week[2] with my friend Mr. Hope[3]—on business. In that case, naturally you will see me, if you will be so kind. I shall not inflict myself for long. A visit of two or three hours—what do you say?!

Meanwhile I embrace you heartily, kiss your hands, and am ever your most devoted nephew,

J. C. Korzeniowski.

1. In Brussels. See L. 11, n. 3.
2. But cf. L. 13.
3. G. F. W. Hope, Director of the South African Mercantile Co. (*LF*, p. 27). (Note "the Director of Companies" in "H. of D.," p. 45.) It was to Hope and his wife that *Lord Jim* (1900) was dedicated, "with grateful affection after many years of friendship." See also Jessie Conrad, *C. as I Knew Him*, pp. 41 f.

13. London, 17 February 1891.

[*Printed letterhead:*[1] The British and Foreign Transit Agency. From Barr, Moering & Co., Shipping and Custom House Agents, Offices: 36, Camomile Street, London, E.C.]

17 Feb., [18]91.

My dear Aunt,

What do you think! I have been in Scotland[2]—still on business. I have just read your dear letters. You are the most excellent of Aunts!—I am a little tired and my legs are swollen once more. I intend to rest for several days.—The trip to Antwerp is put off for some time, or perhaps entirely given up so far as business is concerned. But that will not keep me from coming to Brussels shortly—to pay you a little visit. Please drop me a line on receipt of this scrawl to tell me how you are. I must hurry home[3] to lie down; that is why I don't write at greater length.

A hearty embrace.

Your very grateful and devoted nephew,

K. N. Korzeniowski.

I shall soon write a long letter.

14. London, 27 February 1891.

27 Feb., 1891.

Dear Aunt,

Ill in bed in hospital.[1] Rheumatism in left leg and neuralgia in right arm. Thanks for your kindnesses. Will write as soon as possible.

I embrace you.

J. Conrad.

1. This and the other letterheads of Barr, Moering & Co. that appear in this correspondence are not presented in full. It is also to be noted that the heads of the three letters in App. I have "188" as the fixed part of the year-date; that the present letter has "18"; and that the others have "189."

2. In Glasgow, seeking a command (*LL*, I, 144).

3. He was probably now residing in Greenhithe. See Jessie Conrad, *C. as I Knew Him*, p. 101.

---

1. The German Hospital in London (Jessie Conrad, *C. and His Circle*, p. 13).

27.7ber 1891

Chère Tante

Malade au lit à l'hôpital. Rheumatisme de jambe gauche et neuralgie de bras droit. Merci pour vos bontés. Aussitot possible écrirais. ——

Je vous embrasse

J. Conrad

Letter 14

15. London, 12 March 1891.

In pencil.

12 Mar., '91.

Dear Aunt,

Still in bed. Legs in bad condition and stomach too. Thanks for your letters. I am very uneasy about your relapses.

I am not in a very cheerful mood.

A hearty embrace.

J. Conrad.

16. London, 30 March 1891.

30 Mar., 1891. London.

My dear Aunt,

I have just got up; I have finished a letter to my uncle, and a second one (this) is of course for you. I am quite worried to learn you are suffering with laryngitis. You must be very cautious with that; all those maladies unfortunately drag on, and I fully realize your impatience. I have been in bed for a month, and I believe it the longest month of my life—and I am still not well, far from it, though a good deal better.

Thanks, thanks, for your letters. It is a joy for me to receive them. In the pleasure of reading them I forget (egoist that I am) what effort they must have cost you to write when you are so ill. Did you not go out too soon, dear Aunt? It is abominable weather here.

Thanks to your inexhaustible kindness to me, the shipowners of the United Kingdom have bestirred themselves. I have received a letter from Mr. Knott[1] of Newcastle, who, at the request of M. Pécher, is making overtures to me regarding the command of a steamer. Unfortunately, in the present circumstances I cannot take advantage of his kindly disposition towards me. I have not yet written to thank M. Pécher, for writing tires me too much. In a few days we shall see. Let me have news of you when possible.

1. Of the "Prince" Steam Shipping Co., Ltd. For both Mr. Knott and M. Pécher, see L. 11, n. 4.

Provided that it be good news! I have had an invitation from my uncle[2]—the dear man.

A hearty embrace.

Your devoted nephew and servant,

CONRAD KORZENIOWSKI.

My respects to your mother and sister-in-law.

17. LONDON, 14 APRIL 1891.

14 Apr., '91.

Dear Aunt,

Ever and ever so many thanks for your letter. How tired you must be! I am very sorry and uneasy about your sister-in-law's health. I view everything with such discouragement—everything darkly. My nerves are completely disordered.

So poor Uncle Jean[1] is dead! What a sad end! I surely must write to dear Aunt Gaba, but I haven't the courage to do it. The truth is that the effort of gathering my ideas together and finding the Polish for them is, for the present, beyond me.

Drop me a line, dear Aunt, if you have time. Don't tire yourself with writing at length. Just a postcard to let me know how things are with you.

My respects to your mother.

I embrace you and kiss your hands.

Your very devoted nephew,

C. KORZENIOWSKI.

18. LONDON, 1 MAY 1891.

1 May, 1891. London.

Dearest Aunt,

I received your letter of the 21st some days ago but was

2. Who had written to C. twice during this month. See *LL*, II, 358.

1. Jean Zagórski. See L. 3 and App. IV.

not well enough to answer it. The fact is, my nerves are out of hand, causing heart palpitations and fits of stifling. It is apparently not dangerous, but it is very hard to bear and weakens me greatly.

I think that about the end of May I am going to enter a hydropathic institution near Geneva.[1] In that case I shall be passing through Paris, where I shall have the pleasure of seeing you. I beg you not to write my uncle about my health. I shall write him myself next week. Please forgive these so stupid letters of mine. The ones from you are my joy. Don't be discouraged; write—in so doing you will perform a good and charitable deed. Your letters are positively stimulating, and that is what I require. Your egoistic nephew embraces you heartily.

J. C. Korzeniowski.

19. London, 10 May 1891.

10 May, 1891. London.

My dear Aunt,

I received with joy (as always) your letter of 3 May. You don't state when you are leaving Lille[1] for good. I am accordingly sending this letter to the Rue de la Barre, and I have no doubt that it will be forwarded if you are already in Paris.

I plan to leave here the 17th, next Sunday; so the 18th I shall probably be in Paris. I don't know what route I shall take; probably Folkestone-Boulogne.

I shall stop in Paris only one day—this time. On returning I shall arrange to stop a little longer if you are still there. Your letter pleases me with the tone of hope and of interest in life I find in it. Day is beginning to dawn for you, and I hope—I wish with all my heart, with all my soul—that you may realize all your dreams, see all your desires fulfilled.

1. The Hôtel-Pension de la Roseraie, at Champel. It is described in *LL*, I, 145.

---

1. Where she had relatives, her father having lived in Lille prior to going to Brussels in 1835 (*Biog. nat. de Belgique*, VII, 406).

I am still plunged in deepest night, and my dreams are only nightmares; I have, however, been stifling less for several days. One must not complain.

A hearty embrace. Your very devoted nephew,

K. N. KORZENIOWSKI.

20. CHAMPEL, SWITZERLAND, 28 MAY 1891.

Despite the "1892" in the body of the letter, 1891 is clearly correct. The paper (App. V, no. 6), often found from 15 May, 1890 (L. 7) to 8 July, 1891 (L. 25), then disappears from this correspondence. The handwriting is closely similar to that of the letters bearing dates in the spring and summer of 1891. The content of the letter proper strongly favors a position somewhat prior to L. 21 (dated 3 June, 1891). But the most definite and conclusive evidence is afforded by the postscript. In 1892, C. enjoyed relatively good health and was, during most of the year, at sea (Lrs. 34 ff.); in 1891, in late May, he made the first of his visits to a hydropathic hospital at Champel (Lrs. 18 ff.).

The Thursday of the heading was in all probability his second at Champel; that is, 28 May. See n. 4.

Thursday evening.

My very dear and good Aunt,

I have meditated long on the contents of your letter, and unhappily without coming to any conclusion. I do not doubt that you would have allowed me to give my opinion as to your place of residence, but I must admit my incompetence to form one. The Princess' plan[1] does not displease me, but I know you (a little) and am very much afraid you will not accept it. You are just a tiny bit *impraticable,*[2] my dear Aunt. Though I deplore this, I own it is only one more charm your dear self has for me. Yet, having so many others, you could very well do without this one and let yourself be guided (for once in your life) by the light of pure reason, which resembles that of electricity in being cold. But in the year of grace 1892[3] it is too late to return to the

1. The details of this plan are necessarily conjectural. Perhaps, as has been suggested in L. 4, n. 4, the Princess had asked Mme. P. to live at least part of the year with her. The only thing certain, however, is that Mme. P. decided to live alone in Passy. See Lrs. 21, 24, 33, and 37.

2. Not underlined by C. but placed in quotation marks.

3. See the introductory note.

noble twopenny candle of our ancestors. In the meanwhile I shall be uneasy until I have had another letter.

A hearty embrace.

Your devoted nephew and servant,

CONRAD.

Cure begun two days ago,[4] so cannot yet judge the results. I am bearing it well enough.

21. CHAMPEL, 3 JUNE 1891.

Wednesday, 3 June, 1891. La Roseraie, Geneva.

My dear Aunt,

I have read your latest letter with joy. At last you are perfect, for you are letting yourself be guided by reason.[1] I embrace you heartily for this. Everything will be all right; I have the strongest presentiment that success awaits you. The Princess is very kind, but in loving you she does no more than her duty, I think—and besides, she simply couldn't help it!

My return is a little uncertain. In any case I could spend only a day in Paris, and for those few hours it does not seem wise to disturb you. You will need rest in the country before going to work in Paris. I have an idea that in any event we shall soon see each other again. I feel much better, if not entirely cured.—I have written my uncle several times but have long been without news of him.[2]

I embrace you heartily, congratulating you on your success. Your very devoted nephew and servant,

J. CONRAD.

If you have time to drop me a line you will make me very happy.

4. Apparently 26 May, for in *LL,* I, 145, C.'s arrival at Champel is dated Thursday, 21 May, in accordance with the records of the establishment; and this, if correct, precludes the possibility that this Thursday was the one of the letter itself.

---

1. In arriving at the decision to reside alone in Paris. See Lrs. 24, 33, and 37.
2. His uncle's last letter was evidently one dated 12 Apr. See *LL,* II, 358.

22. Champel, 10 June 1891.

Wednesday, 10 June, '91.

Dear Aunt,

Thanks for your kind and charming letter. I was serious about Paris, and I am likewise very serious in letting you know that I shall arrive there the 15th of this month (Monday) in the morning, to leave in the evening.

So about ten-thirty I shall be at your door, as you intend to return to Paris the 14th.

I love and embrace you heartily.

Your very devoted nephew,

J. C. Korzeniowski.

I am fairly well.

23. London, 22 June 1891.

22 June, 1891. London.

My dearest Aunt,

I have not written you sooner because I had truly nothing to say. Last Thursday[1] I went aboard my friend Hope's yacht,[2] and I have returned to London just this moment; or hardly two hours ago, to be exact.

My health is pretty fair, though I am not yet very strong. The little cruise in the yacht did me much good.

I am forming vague plans for the future; very vague! Yet what good is it to plan, since it is always the unforeseen that happens? As soon as the said unforeseen does happen, I shall write you an account of it. I am myself rather curious to discover what it will be like.

Drop me a line, dear Aunt, when you have time, and forgive me these so uninteresting letters.

I embrace you heartily. Your very devoted nephew,

J. C. Korzeniowski.

1. The 18th.
2. Probably "La Reine." See Jessie Conrad, *C. and His Circle,* pp. 53 and 74 f. Also note *LL,* II, 143, and "H. of D.," pp. 45 ff.

24. London, 2 July 1891.

2 July, 1891.

Dear Aunt,

Thanks for your kind letter. How happy I am to know you are settled somewhere! Truly I did not like to think of you in the doctor's apartment. It was too nightmarish with those paintings of the Charenton[1] school and that little bell! One may well laugh at the whole thing for a while, but after all it ends by becoming painful. I am so glad to know you are about satisfied. I want terribly to dash to Passy to see the apartment[2] (don't go thinking for a moment it would be to see you!) and once there (in the apartment) to eat the dinner the menu of which is already occupying your thoughts. (And mine too, moreover.) Frankly, your letter made me happy. Its tone was so good. And, above all, no discouragement!

My health is passable. I leave tomorrow in Hope's yacht for the East Coast. We return next Monday.[3]

All my plans have miscarried. So I am making no more. One cannot avoid his destiny. We shall see what it brings. I embrace you heartily.

Your

Conrad.

25. London, 8 July 1891.

8 July, 1891.

Dear Aunt,

I have just read your letter with sorrow and indignation. Indignation against the injustice of the suffering that pursues you, against the cruelty of things and the brutality of the inevitable—since everything is inevitable! And in the case of accidents like that of which your cousin[1] has just been the unfortunate victim, the sorrow is more poignant

1. The well-known insane asylum near Paris.

2. At 84 Rue de Passy. (This is the address on a number of the envelopes preserved in the collection.) Mme. P. was to reside here for many years. See L. 106.

3. The 6th.

---

1. The editors have been unable to discover who this was.

and the regret more bitter. For here there is always the thought of what might have been, the regret for things unaccomplished, the despair over the useless sacrifice of a love on which depended the happiness of those who remain stunned with astonishment at the inexplicable cruelty of the Invisible that guides inanimate things to destroy a life necessary to the happiness of innocent beings, of that being not yet conscious! Truly we are the slaves of fate before our birth, and we pay tribute to misfortune before we have known what it is. Does it, I fearfully ask myself, follow us beyond the tomb?

But if there is anyone in the world to console bruised hearts, it is indeed you. You who have passed through the ordeal by fire. You who have known how to bear courageously not only death, but even life. Happy in their misfortune are those to whom your gracious and bountiful heart bears consolation, those whose wounds are dressed by your hand, grown expert by cruel experience. There are others who must suffer and bleed in mute solitude! They are to be pitied. You know that yourself, alas!

I am sorry to have been away when your letter arrived. I admire and love you more and more.

I kiss your hands.

J. C. KORZENIOWSKI.

26. LONDON, 22 JULY 1891.

[*Engraved letterhead:* The British and Foreign Transit Agency. Barr, Moering & Co. Offices, 36, Camomile Street, London E.C.]

22 July, [189]1.

My dear Aunt,

I have just received your letter containing the map as well as poor Jeannette's[1] death-certificate.[2] I cannot pretend to a great sorrow; the fact is that this death is a relief to everyone, including the deceased.

1. Mme. P.'s sister-in-law. See L. 3 and App. IV.

2. The French reads, *le passport mortuaire.* In a Russian funeral the priest provided a death-certificate with his and another clergyman's signatures, and this was often referred to as the deceased's "passport to heaven" (*NED,* under "passport," 2, c).

By all means do accept the Ordęgas'[3] invitation. I am sure it will do you good, for you need something of the sort to restore you after your days in the hospital. As for me, I am rather busy, and yachting[4] is out of the question.

All my plans have failed and I believe I shall have to remain in London for good. No time to explain today. I shall write soon.

I embrace you and kiss your hands.

Your very devoted

J. CONRAD.

27. LONDON, 30 JULY 1891.

30 July, 1891. London.

Aunt dearest,

Here I am, ill again—just as I was about to begin work![1] An attack of malaria in the shape of dyspepsia. It is discouraging.

I don't know what to say to you, for I can't think. I am stunned by this new disaster—for such it is for me under the circumstances.

Drop me a line.

A hearty embrace.

J. CONRAD.

28. LONDON, 5 AUGUST 1891.

5/8/91. London.

My dear Aunt,

Thanks for your kind letter, but why are you alarmed? I am perhaps a little to blame. I am always complaining and groaning, and my Aunt takes me seriously.

I began work yesterday. For the time being I am in charge of the warehouse of Messrs. Barr, Moering.[1]

3. In the summer of 1939 Mlle. Aniela Zagórska kindly wrote the editors from Warsaw that she knew of this family and would send what information she could gather. But the invasion of Poland intervened.

4. The word is in English.

---

1. See L. 28.

---

1. See the letterhead to L. 29.

If I see that I can accustom myself to this life, I shall remain in London.

I still have a little fever every day; nothing serious, only it keeps me from regaining my strength. Accordingly I get tired very quickly. I beg you not to write all this to my uncle. I intend to write him in two or three days to announce the recovery along with the illness.

I kiss your hands.

Yours,

J. CONRAD.

29. LONDON, 26 AUGUST 1891.

The date, which appears only on the second sheet, was first written as 25 Aug.

[*Printed letterhead:* Barr, Moering & Co., Dyers' Hall Wharf, (Warehouses, Nos. 1 & 2) 95, Upper Thames Street, London, E.C.]

26 Aug., [189]1.

My dearest Aunt,

Thanks for your kind letter, which I received the day before yesterday.

My health is not exactly radiant, but on the whole I don't feel badly, despite an occasional touch of fever. I am writing to you here in the vast (and dusty) solitude of this warehouse, as I have a free moment about the middle of the day. In the evening, back home again, I feel so lazy that I look upon pens with horror; and as for the inkwell, I have banished it from my room long since.

After all, I am not so happy to be working as you seem to think. There is nothing very exhilarating in doing disagreeable work. It is too much like penal servitude, with the difference that while rolling the stone of Sisyphus[1] you lack the consolation of thinking of what pleasure you had in committing the crime. It is here that convicts have the advantage over your humble servant.

I am very vexed that my uncle should have taken it upon himself to join the others[2] in annoying you. At least you

1. Note a similar allusion in *LL*, II, 36.

2. Evidently her relatives in Poland, in that Thadée Bobrowski has become involved. (See also n. 4.)

may be assured that his motives are less mercenary than you imagine. As for myself, I believe those questions to be so personal that I cannot take much interest in them, even when they concern those nearest me. Even if a sister were involved I do not think I could entertain a real interest. Which does not prevent my thinking (at the risk of displeasing you forever) that the person who has had the bad luck to offend you so is a very fine fellow.[3] One admires what one lacks. That is why I admire perseverance and fidelity and constancy. And then I like to look on the good side of men, particularly if there is a suggestion of pathos in the situation. That completes the affair from the artistic point of view, which is mine in this business. You seem not to be conscious of the characteristic note of sadness of life in all this episode. The weary yet hopeful waiting and the hopeless collapse at the end.[4] But after all, on thinking of it, it is perhaps not sad; it is perhaps quite—funny?[5] Still, I don't know! You see I am discussing all this academically. And for the last time.

What really interests me is your new work.[6] I am waiting for it impatiently, but meanwhile let me know in what number of the *Figaro illustré*[7] you are appearing and also the date of the *Revue*. I wish you success with all my heart; you are not lacking in courage, and happiness will come with work. Amen!

I embrace you and kiss your hands.

Yours,

J. CONRAD.

I beg you not to spare us. It will do them good back there to see something of what they are like. Perhaps?! Although

3. The last three words are in English.

4. The words from "of the characteristic" to "end" inclusive are in English. To what episode they refer is uncertain, but it may be guessed that it involved her exiled husband's patrimony. (See L. 5 and L. 39, n. 1.)

5. A similar comment, though of more general application, occurs in *PR*, p. xviii, ll. 22 ff.

6. See L. 30, n. 1.

7. Apparently C. has confused the *Figaro illustré*, which contains nothing by her, and the *Figaro* ("Supplément littéraire"). See Lrs. 39, 40, and 45, n. 4.

curing madmen with literature seems a little improbable. What do you think? And then it will please M. Buloz[8] and the Russians and help along the Grand Alliance.[9]

30. London, 15 September 1891.

15 Sept., 1891. London.

My dearest Aunt,

Thanks for your letter and the *Revue,* which I received two days ago. I have read "La Madone"[1] and consider myself lucky to have read it in French and in your adaptation, for I think it must be rather tiresome in Polish if Łozinski, like the others, has the habit of "marking time," as you put it. Naturally I do not find in it the "relief," the clear-cut life, of *Yaga,* but I have again found with great delight the language, the style, and, in short, almost all the purely literary pleasure the reading of *Yaga* gave me. The fact is that, with my hunger aroused (if I may so express myself), I have just reread *Yaga,* which I like more than ever.

I shall give close heed from now on to what I say to you or write you if you adopt the bad habit of remembering my words. Your sympathy is very dear to me, but to speak truly I don't care a straw for happiness. I hardly know what it is. I am no more courageous or independent than anyone else; I am perhaps more indifferent, which is not a virtue, though likewise not a defect. Why should you be unhappy? Why should it be good for you to be so, and bad for me? We are ordinary people who have just the happiness we deserve; no more, no *less.* If I occasionally let you glimpse that life is sometimes painful to me, this is a weakness on my part of which I am very ashamed. But you must not take me too seriously. I bear quite well on my shoulders

8. Charles Buloz (1843–1905), who in 1877 succeeded his father, François, as editor of *RDM,* holding this position until 1893, when F. Brunetière assumed it. See *Larousse du XXe siècle,* I, 910.

9. This postscript seems to refer to her forthcoming "Popes et popadias" (see L. 41, n. 1), which offers the suggestion that Galicia and the Ukraine be united (with Kiev as capital) and accuses the Poles of having allowed their nobility to lie dormant (Pt. XV).

---

1. "La Madone de Busowiska," from the Polish of Ladislas Łozinski (1843–1912). It appeared in *RDM* for 1 Sept., 1891.

the burden of the whole world, as do likewise the five million miserable creatures who make up the population of this city. You know very well that I am not complaining. I am telling you only what I feel, relying on your friendship.

Oh, my dear Aunt, "Men are incredible" (speaking of convicts), and I would say to you that women are . . . very womanly.

But, my dear Aunt, if these convicts found solace in expiation they would no longer be convicts but angels (Catholic angels) fallen into misfortune. Being convicts they find their solace in the memory of crimes committed and in the anticipation of crimes to be committed once the penalty is paid. Convicts are a very ill-appreciated class of people. They have all the virtues of their defects. The only class above them is that one (small in number) of persons who have committed crimes without allowing themselves to be caught.

After all, how little does one know oneself! I astonish and perhaps scandalize you by my joking about criminals, while you think me capable of accepting or even admitting the doctrine (or theory) of expiation through suffering. That doctrine, a product of superior but savage minds, is quite simply an infamous abomination when preached by civilized people. It is a doctrine which, on the one hand, leads straight to the Inquisition and, on the other, discloses the possibilities of bargaining with the Eternal. It would be quite as rational to wish to expiate a murder by a theft! "Two wrongs cannot make a right."[2] Moreover, there is no expiation. Each act of life is final and inevitably produces its consequences in spite of all the weeping and gnashing of teeth and the sorrow of weak souls who suffer as fright grips them when confronted with the results of their own actions. As for myself, I shall never need to be consoled for any act of my life, and this because I am strong enough to judge my conscience rather than be its slave, as the orthodox would like to persuade us to be.

Pardon all this nonsense. Though fallen into complete destitution I am not yet reduced to living in the Company's offices. So my private address is not Camomile Street but

2. In English.

17 Gillingham Street,[3] S.W.—though as I am soon going to move, you would do better to write me at the office, as usual. —My respects to your mother. I embrace you heartily.

J. Conrad.

31. London, 30 September 1891.

30 Sept., 1891. 17 Gillingham St., London, S.W.

My dear Aunt,

I should have thanked you long since for your kind and charming letter. You flatter me in it (which is always pleasant); and you are happy because I have read *Yaga;* and you have such a pretty dream—that of your devoted nephew arriving in Passy. Dreams are helpful sometimes; one forgets.

It is extremely probable that I shall soon embark on a long voyage; Australia or elsewhere, it matters little to me. I am taking the necessary steps and am pleased to believe they will lead to something.

I shall be gone for no more than a year (discounting the unforeseen), and on my return I shall set about making your dream a reality. Oh, what a lovely dream! A lovely dream!

All this is only tentative, you well understand, but I shall keep you informed of what is happening. Just now my head is so empty (except for the above plans) that I dare scribble no more. I have noticed that when one has nothing to say, one always says too much; consequently I close. I present my respects to your mother, and I embrace you and kiss your hands.

Wholly yours,

J. Conrad.

32. London, 16 October 1891.

The year is almost certainly 1891. The tone and substance of the letter are in keeping with the philosophical and highly subjective meditations in his other letters of this period (see *LL,* I, 147 f.), and its paper (App. V,

3. In Pimlico, near Victoria Station.

no. 12) is that of Lrs. 30 f., which is found nowhere else in this correspondence except once again in 1906.

16 Oct. London. 17 Gillingham St., S.W.

Dear Aunt,

I am wondering if you are very angry with your most lazy nephew? I like to think, however, that you recognize the duty of leniency, since life is possible only by virtue of that recognition.

I have absolutely nothing to tell you. I am vegetating. I don't even think; therefore I don't exist (according to Descartes). But another person (a learned man) has said: "No thought without phosphorus." Whence it seems to be the phosphorus that is absent, while as for me, I am still here. But in that case I should be existing without thinking, which (according to Descartes) is impossible. Good heavens, could I be a Punch? The Punch of my childhood, you know, with his spine broken in two and his nose on the floor between his feet; his legs and arms stiffly spread, in that attitude of deep despair—so pathetically comic—of toys thrown in a corner. He had no phosphorus; I know, for I licked all the paint from his scarlet cheeks, kissed, and even bit, his nose many times without being any the worse for it. He was a true friend. He heard my secrets sympathetically, regarding me with an affectionate eye. I say "an" eye because in the first days of our friendship I had put out the other one in a fit of mad tenderness. Yet he seemed never to give it any thought, for fear of causing me pain. He was a gentleman.[1] Other Punches that I have known since then have cried when their toes were stepped on. Did you ever hear of such impertinence!? After all, nothing can take the place of our childhood affections.

This evening I feel as if I were in a corner, spine broken, nose in the dust. Will you have the kindness to pick up the poor little devil, put him gently in your apron, introduce him to your dolls, let him play at dinners with the others? I can see myself now at the feast, nose smeared with jam, the others looking at me with that expression of frigid astonishment characteristic of well-made dolls. I have many

1. The last word is in English.

times been thus looked at by countless manikins! Upon my word, I pardon them; once upon a time I was a Christian!

I had intended, on beginning this letter, to tell you that I like your costume (for the portrait),[2] though it is difficult for me to imagine you in it. Do you know that by one of those charming jokes in which Destiny abounds, I have never seen you but in black? Well, *qui vivra verra.* Perhaps I shall live long enough to see your portrait.

A hearty embrace. Your very devoted

J. CONRAD.

33. LONDON, 22 OCTOBER 1891.

[*Printed letterhead* (*as in L. 29*): Barr, Moering & Co., Dyers' Hall Wharf, (Warehouses, Nos. 1 & 2) 95, Upper Thames Street, London, E.C.]

22 Oct., [189]1.

Dearest Aunt,

I received your letter just this morning as I was going out. I brought it along in my pocket, read it on the train, and am answering at once. If your letter is "boring," as you call it, I like to be bored; if it is "inept," please heaven the mantle of that ineptness may fall on my shoulders! If it is "stupid," then it is a stupidity worth a million bits of wisdom. Your letter is so human in that sadness of all beginnings.[1] I understand you perfectly. It is the hesitation at the threshold, the aversion to strange things, the uncertainty of the darkness in which one gropes in fear. But you will see. Solitude loses its terrors when one knows it; it is a tribulation which, for the courageous who have lifted the cup to their lips without flinching, becomes a sweetness whose charm would not be exchanged for anything else in the whole world.

So, without flinching, drink; and courage will come with the forgetfulness, or rather the obliteration, of the past. It is not the lack of a fire in the middle room that discourages

2. For further details concerning this portrait, see L. 75, n. 5.

1. In reference to her new experience of living by herself. See Lrs. 21, 24, and 37.

you; you doubt unknowingly the divine spark that is in you. In this you are like everyone else. Will you be different from everyone and have that faith which fans the spark into a bright fire? From the bottom of my heart, dear Aunt, I believe you will! Do not come down from the pedestal where I have set you, even though that would mean to come nearer me. I am not always an egoist. A hearty embrace. Will write soon.

J. Conrad.

34. London, 14 November 1891.

14 Nov., 1891. 36 Camomile St., London, E.C.

My dearest Aunt,

It is first of all to you that I send news of my approaching departure. It happened all of a sudden. Yesterday afternoon I had a letter from an acquaintance of mine in command of the ship "Torrens," offering me the berth of first officer.[1] I accepted, and today (at seven-thirty in the morning) I took over from my predecessor. It is now after ten in the evening. I have just come back to my new lodgings near the dock[2] where the ship is. I am rather worn out from my long day's work and feel very inclined to go to bed, but . . . it is first of all to you that must be sent the great news.

We leave in six days[3] and are far from ready for this. From next Monday[4] on we shall probably work day and night, so I shall be very busy. This may be my last letter from London. The ship is bound for Port Adelaide (South Australia). The passage will be from seventy to eighty days.[5] I shall write on arrival, and the letter, going by mail-steamer through the Suez Canal, will be forty days in

1. See C.'s "The 'Torrens': A Personal Tribute," pp. 26 f. The captain was Walter H. Cope. An account (with two pictures) of this famous ship is in Lubbock, *The Colonial Clippers*, pp. 157–162.

2. In the London Dock system. See Tomlinson, *Below London Bridge*, pp. 2 f.; "The 'Torrens': A Personal Tribute," p. 26; "Ocean Travel," p. 37; and *LL*, II, 333.

3. C. signed the ship's articles on 20 Nov., and on 25 Nov. the "Torrens" left Plymouth (*LL*, I, 149).

4. The 16th.

5. But see the opening words and n. 1 of L. 35.

transit. Let's say, then, that in four months you will have news of me.

During this period you will remember me kindly, will keep a place for me in your heart; and on my return (in nine or ten months) we shall try to see each other, if you like. But what good are plans? Destiny is our master!

I kiss both your hands and embrace you heartily.

J. CONRAD.

If you reply at once to the address in the heading, you will find me still here.

Australian address: Mr. *J. Conrad,* Chief mate, Ship "Torrens," Pt. Adelaide, South Australia.[6] (Write in mid-January.)

35. PORT ADELAIDE, 5 MARCH 1892.

5 Mar., 1892. Ship "Torrens," Port Adelaide.

My dearest Aunt,

We arrived here the day before yesterday[1] after a long voyage. I sprang upon your letters, and I hasten to thank you for the pleasure I had in reading them.

But nothing is all pleasure in this world; the news of your health disturbs me. I don't like that persistent bronchitis, and I am afraid you are carrying the spirit of self-sacrifice too far. For it is clear that you are not taking enough care of yourself—perhaps none at all.

I must also admit that I understand imperfectly—perhaps not at all—the line of conduct you have chosen. I cannot imagine on what ethical grounds you base your conduct towards your aunt.[2] I suppose family feeling enters into it, but I view all this differently. As I look at it, the rights and duties of such a relationship are mutual, while here it

6. The address is in English.

---

1. According to Lubbock the "Torrens" arrived at Port Adelaide on 28 Feb. (*The Colonial Clippers,* p. 162). Because of his thoroughness in checking such dates (see *ibid.,* p. vii) and of C.'s having elsewhere evidently used the expression "the day before yesterday" carelessly (see L. 9, introd.), the date as given by Lubbock need not be seriously questioned.
2. It has not been possible to identify her more precisely.

seems to me that you have all the duties and your aunt all the rights—if we admit that one human being may have the right physically or morally to wound another, which I cannot admit. In my circle, family feeling manifests itself in a complete solidarity among all the members, which sanctions by approval all the acts of individuals—so long as these acts are not dishonorable. But the individual's right to order his life as he pleases is never put in question to satisfy the demands of a more or less trifling egoism. Respect for age doubtless enters into it too. But please remember that old age is a misfortune, not a privilege; that wisdom, whatever one may say, does not increase with the number of years; that the respect due old age is really at bottom only a veiled feeling of deep pity for the unhappy creatures whom death has forgotten but whom time has robbed of hope. Your aunt doubtless possesses all the virtues which are the Creator's universal gift to mankind—but not Charity, which is a gift straight from the Eternal to the elect. For Charity is eternal and universal Love, the divine virtue, the sole manifestation of the Almighty which may in some manner justify the act of creation.

Hence, the longing for self-sacrifice, for returning good for evil—that mysterious urge towards abnegation and suffering which guides womanly feeling—is the principal reason for your conduct, in appearance so highly exemplary, towards your aunt. Unfortunately I cannot lay at your feet the tribute of admiration which you have, at first sight, so richly deserved; for in my opinion abnegation carried to an extreme—where you are carrying it—becomes not a fault but a crime, and to return good for evil is not only profoundly immoral but dangerous, in that it sharpens the appetite for evil in the malevolent and develops (perhaps unconsciously) that latent human tendency towards hypocrisy in the . . . let us say, benevolent.

Moreover, it seems to me in this affair that, with your desire to perform your duty towards your aunt, you have failed in your duty to yourself. You have thrown aside dignity, affections, memories! And why? Have you found the peace which is the reward of sacrifices accepted by the Master of our souls?

I tell you all this because I love you dearly, admire you immensely; and I kiss your hands in saying au revoir—if you still wish to see me on my return.

Your very devoted nephew,

J. CONRAD KORZENIOWSKI.

We leave here 10 April.[3] If you write to

Mr. J. Conrad,
Chief officer,
Ship "Torrens,"
Cape Town,[4]

where we are to arrive about the end of May, you will make me happy. I am very busy. I will write you from here before we depart. My compliments to your mother and sister-in-law.

36. PORT ADELAIDE, 6 APRIL 1892.

6 Apr., 1892. On board the "Torrens," Port Adelaide.

My dearest Aunt,

We leave tomorrow for the Cape of Good Hope, from where we shall go to St. Helena and then to London. I expect to be in Europe about mid-August,[1] if all goes well.

I have been terribly busy during our stay here; this, along with a sort of mental torpor which depresses me, has prevented my writing you more often. This is my third,[2] and last, letter from Australia. I am counting on your indulgence. Moreover, you know very well that if I don't write often, I love you none the less for that.

Your letters have been delightful—interesting and unusual—for it has been your lot to meet characters not ordinarily found on the road of life we simple mortals travel—

I have just been interrupted. I resume: I mean that you have the author's eye, one that sees characteristics unno-

3. Cf., however, the opening words of L. 36 (and also *LL*, I, 149, n. 3).
4. The address is in English.

1. But see the opening words and n. 1 of L. 37.
2. Mme. P. has penciled "a letter lost" above the salutation.

ticed by those whose business is not that of observing their fellows. Yet there are those who can observe well enough but cannot describe. You both observe and describe. In the [—][3] and striking simplicity of your descriptions you remind me a little of Flaubert, whose *Mme. Bovary* I have just reread[4] with respectful admiration—

I have been interrupted again. I resume: There you have a man with enough imagination for two realists. There are few authors so creative as he. One never questions for a moment either his characters or his episodes; one would doubt rather one's own existence. So much for Flaubert.

Your health makes me uneasy, dear Aunt. I should much like to have had a reassuring letter from you before sailing. The mail-boat arrived yesterday. Nothing! I resign myself, but am none the happier for doing so.—Nothing from my uncle, but at least his last letter contained good news.

I am afraid of having displeased you in my first letter.[5] You must pardon me. You realize very well that if I did not love you so dearly I should not so bitterly resent the unhappy ironies of your existence. It is my right to be angry when I see a heart that is in my opinion worthy of a better fate wear itself out in a struggle against troubles, against the quirks of destiny, floundering in a stream of which the source is the ruthless egoism of hearts inferior to the one they victimize. That is why I took the liberty of telling you that, in this particular case, self-sacrifice is a fault and almost a crime. But why expatiate on that!? Women don't understand these things. I could preach till doomsday. I fume, am silent, and admire.

I kiss your hands. Good-bye for a little while.

Your wholly devoted

J. Conrad.

Write to London, care of Messrs. Barr, Moering, 36 Camomile Street, E.C.

3. Beginning a new page, C. has omitted a word.

4. C. was later to declare that he had not read Flaubert until after he had completed *AF* (*LL*, II, 206).

5. That is, L. 35. (See *supra*, p. 43, n. 2.)

37. London, 4 September 1892.

4 Sept., 1892. London.

Dearest Aunt,

I arrived the day before yesterday[1] and had the pleasure of reading your charming and kind letters this morning. I found them all in London, for, as my friend Krieger[2] was very seriously ill, no one at the office had sense enough to forward them to me in Australia or at the Cape, where they knew perfectly well we were going to put in. I am glad to learn of your (comparative) happiness, or at least of the peace you have found in that solitude you so dreaded. Unfortunately I must tell you that I shall be unable to disturb that solitude, for I shall be very busy, with leave entirely out of the question. And as for resigning from the ship, I cannot afford that luxury on account of my daily bread—you know, that which one eats by the sweat of one's brow, and sometimes by the sweat of another's when one is clever enough to stay in the shade and let others strive in the sun. As for me, I have neither that cleverness nor that luck, so you will not see me in Passy this year. I tell you this at once, for I believe you capable of upsetting all your plans for your worth-nothing (not "good-for-nothing")[3] nephew.

I am saddened by what you tell me of Jean.[4] You are thinking already of his future conquests and of the hearts he will break. How characteristic that is, individually and nationally! For my part, I think that, reared in that fashion, he will grow up and reach maturity without realizing the meaning of life and with a false notion of his place in the world. He will think himself important. One always thinks himself important at twenty. The fact is, however, that one becomes useful only on realizing the utter insignificance of the individual in the scheme of the universe. When one well understands that in oneself one is nothing and that a man is worth neither more nor less than the work he accomplishes with honesty of purpose and means, and

1. C.'s discharge was issued on 3 Sept. (Keating, *C. Mem. Lib.*, p. 401).
2. Of Barr, Moering & Co. See L. 11, n. 11. *Tales of Unrest* (1898) was dedicated to him, "for the sake of old days."
3. C. is punning upon *vaut-rien* and *vaurien*.
4. Her nephew.

within the strict limits of his duty towards society, only then is one the master of his conscience, with the right to call himself a man. Otherwise, were he more attractive than Prince Charming, richer than Midas, wiser than Doctor Faust himself, the two-legged featherless creature is only a despicable thing sunk in the mud of all the passions. I could spoil a great deal of paper on this theme, but you doubtless understand me as well as I do myself, without further explanation.

My uncle was more or less ill all winter. During the summer he felt better, but I am much afraid it won't last. I may be mistaken, though, for I view everything darkly since my health failed. This is stupid, but that's how it is. We have arranged for me to go to Russia next year, and I shall then pass through Paris.[5] So I am hoping to see you at that time. But making plans is a very unprofitable business. It is always the unexpected that happens.

Remember me to your mother and to Mme. and M. Bouillot. I suppose your sister-in-law and the children are now in England.

Ever and ever so many thanks for your kind remembrance of me. I really don't know how I have deserved to be in your good graces, but I accept this privilege as one accepts gifts from heaven—with humble gratitude, with full consciousness of my unworthiness, and without attempting to understand Eternal Wisdom.

Your very devoted

J. CONRAD.

38. LONDON, 13 SEPTEMBER 1892.

13 Sept., 1892. London.

My dear Aunt,

Your April letter reached me only yesterday. It had gone astray somewhere. I hasten to tell you how happy I am to learn that Hachette's offer[1] suits you. You are on the right track, and no one is happier about it than your nephew.

5. But he went instead via Holland (L. 43).

1. Just what this refers to cannot be determined. See Lrs. 41, n. 1, and 51, n. 2.

This note is especially to tell you that. I am very busy. I go to bed late, get up early, and slave at the same dull routine all day long. As a result, I am becoming positively brutish. I embrace you heartily. Drop me a line.

Always your

J. CONRAD.

39. LONDON, 4 OCTOBER 1892.

4.10.92. London.

My dearest Aunt,

I received your letter just this morning and am thoroughly cheered by it, being very happy about your good fortune.[1] At last you have what you deserve! And I, who speak with full knowledge, am sure it comes not a moment too soon.

I ask nothing better than to forget the contents of your letters of last year, for they caused me much worry and vexation; only let me ask you: is it right to forget so? and I wonder: is it possible to forget? Yet it is very sailorlike, this forgetfulness of wrongs, afflictions, and storms. It is also one of the charming qualities of childhood; and now that I think of it, such a lack of memory is even very Christian. Also it is most convenient for that troop of worthies which travels about the world poisoning life to right and left, handing you the cup of gall. "Come drink, miserable sinner. It won't kill you. It will only wring your heart—a mere trifle! Come drink—and forget!"

You drink. You forget. And then it starts again—torment and tears, sobs and revolt, anger and outraged, honest struggle. But memory is short. "Forget!" they shout at you. And the fight ends in a soft crumbling of disappointed hopes, of cheated affections, of righteous indignation that has been outraged, of dignity that has been abandoned, that has been thrown to the winds all for that fatal word uttered with a false semblance of religious feeling. And there you have it. It is you who are right! Let us forget quickly.

1. This probably refers to the outcome of the financial matters (presumably having to do with her exiled husband's patrimony) discussed in L. 29.

My congratulations on the honor that falls to you again of being mounted astride (shocking!)[2] the two years.[3] You will forward me the *Figaro illustré*[4] in Australia, won't you? I will send the address. You must write directly there. I hope, however, to have yet another letter from you before leaving.

My work is not very diversified, but it is none the less demanding. It could not interest you in the slightest. I am pretty well. I kiss your hands and am ever your very devoted

C. K.

40. London, 19 October 1892.

19.10.92. London.

My dearest Aunt,

You are making a little fun of your nephew in comparing him to the late Hamlet (who was mad, I believe). Nevertheless I permit myself to think that apart from his madness he was an entirely worthy person. I am therefore not offended by the comparison. I don't know where you found any indication of my contempt for mankind. This persuades me that, to make a generalization, one may say that even those who know us best know us very little. The philosopher who said "Know thyself" was, I believe, probably tipsy (having supped with Greek damsels—which was one of the philosophic customs of the time), since I cannot admit him to have been stupid. A philosopher cannot be stupid, can he? One quickly gets to know oneself. The difficulty lies in knowing others. I hasten to assure you before my departure (which will occur the twenty-fifth[1] of this month) that I love humanity doubtless as much as you do, but perhaps in a different fashion. Still, you know, a

2. The word is in English.

3. Though not carried out (see L. 41, n. 1), evidently the intention was to publish "Popes et popadias" in installments bridging the New Year. This had been done in *RDM* with her *Demoiselle Micia* in 1888 and 1889 (see L. 10, n. 4).

4. As in L. 29, C. apparently has the wrong publication in mind. Cf. L. 40, where the *Figaro* is requested, and see L. 45, n. 4.

---

1. This date agrees with Lubbock, *The Colonial Clippers,* p. 162.

lot humanity cares! I despise no one, for I don't wish to have the feeling requited. I am not philosophic enough to bear (calmly) the contempt of those not my peers. And note well that the kicks of a donkey's hoof hurt very badly. One of the constant studies of my life has been to avoid them. Please take cognizance by this writing that I respect the Donkey (with a capital D). I seize this occasion to make my profession of faith. Long ears are eternal, the beginning and the end of all things; I find my rest, my peace, in the shadow they cast across the desert of life, and my consolation in the melodious braying of my master! There you are; what else can you expect? One must live when one has had the misfortune to be born.

Next Wednesday[2] will see me on the blue (more or less) sea. We shall arrive at Port Adelaide about mid-January.[3] Write in December to: Mr. J. Conrad, Chief officer, Ship "Torrens," Port Adelaide, South Australia.[4] Tell me what you are doing and so much of what you are thinking as you see fit. Send me the *Figaro* that is to have your work[5] in it.

And ever, and in spite of everything, believe me to be your very sincere admirer and most devoted nephew,

J. Conrad.

41. Port Adelaide, 3 February 1893.

3 Feb., 1893. Port Adelaide. "Torrens."

My dear Aunt,

Thanks for your kind letter and the *Revue*.[1] The news of your success, of the recognition you have won for your talents at the point of your pen,[2] fills me with joy. I, who

2. The 26th.
3. But cf. L. 41, n. 5.
4. The address is in English.
5. "Joujou." See L. 45, n. 4.

1. Containing her "Popes et popadias," which appeared in *RDM* for 15 Nov. and 1 Dec., 1892. It was published in book form (*Les Filles du pope*, Hachette, Paris) in 1893. In 1896 a German translation (*Die Töchter des Popen*) was printed in Dresden.

2. We have been unable to find any particular event that might have called forth this remark. Numerous French Academy awards were announced in *Le Temps* for 25 Nov., 1892, but no prize was then given to Mme. P. Evidently, too, *Les Filles du pope* ("Popes et popadias") was not crowned until 1895 (see L. 90, n. 1).

have always had faith in, and predicted, your success, am very proud yet not at all surprised.

I sprang, so to speak, upon "Popes et popadias" with eagerness and high hopes. With the first lines my hopes were realized—and then very soon surpassed. It is a marvel of observation, giving the keenest pleasure as such without reference to the style, which I dare not judge, though I may say it charmed me. You well know how to describe. From the crossing of the ferry under the sky in which the storm is mounting, I was enraptured by the entire series of scenes that make up your charming novelette. It is in brief narrative (the short story)[3] that the master hand is revealed. I cannot say whether your characters are set in relief. To me they are wholly alive: the priest and his wife, the child going for medicine in the stormy night, the veterinary, the grandmother with the cat—all are clear-cut, moving about and drawing breath in the atmosphere you have created for them, in the midst of the local settings you have depicted. Then too, it is full of charming touches —of subtle observation, of things caught in motion. And the friends of your veterinary who play cards to console him![4] They are delightful!

Your letter has a cheerful tone. Mine would too were it not for my health, which is not blooming. I was very miserable for a fortnight before our arrival here.[5] Mementoes of Africa. Hence I am going to take a week's leave (beginning tomorrow), which I shall spend in the vicinity of Adelaide, where the greater altitude affords a climate much less warm than that of the seaboard.

I have neither plans nor projects. It is quite probable that on my return I shall go to see my uncle; in that case we shall meet again,[6] my dear and good Aunt. If anything prevents it I shall be much disturbed, for I am greatly attached to the idea. I have fondled it for nearly three years; it is the sole trace of color in the uniform grey of existence.

3. This parenthesis, with "the" omitted, is in English.

4. In contrast to the other scenes here referred to, this one occurs towards the end (Pt. XX).

5. On 30 Jan. (Lubbock, *The Colonial Clippers*, p. 162).

6. But cf. L. 43.

And the said existence begins to weary me a little. It is not the present illness (for I feel much better just now) but the uncertainty of the future—or rather the certainty of the "uniform grey" awaiting me—that causes this discouragement. I know very well that what I have just said, and what I feel, lacks dignity; but at least the feeling is genuine. It is not morbid, for I view the situation without any bitterness. Doubtless it would be more dignified to feel this way without breathing a word, but upon my soul one can't remain always perched on the stilts of one's principles. So I have come down to earth, very close to earth, under your friendly eye. All this in confidence.

I kiss your hands and embrace you heartily. Your devoted servant and nephew,

J. CONRAD.

I found only one letter from my uncle. He complains that every effort tires him, but his health is quite tolerable.

42. CAPE TOWN, 17 MAY 1893.

17 May, 1893. Capetown.

My dearest Aunt,

Thanks for the letter in which you scold me for not writing. I presume that by now you have read my first epistle[1] from Port Adelaide, which, by giving you the date of our arrival in the Colonies, explains my long silence.[2]

I have already told you what I think of "Popes et popadias," but I shall sum it up again: it is a little masterpiece. I should much like to read the novel of French life[3] you wish to see crowned, if I rightly understood your letter. And it will be, dear Aunt and faithful friend. You will succeed in everything, for you deserve success.

And each of your triumphs is a joy to me and likewise gratifies my vanity as a prophet of good things; for I have lived with faith in your talents, which the world recognizes only now. Also I have had the good luck to know you before

1. Probably L. 41, but perhaps one that is missing from the collection.

2. Though he had written that he expected to arrive in Port Adelaide "about mid-January" (L. 40), he did not arrive there until the 30th (L. 41, n. 5).

3. *Le Mariage du fils Grandsire.* See L. 51, n. 2.

you and the world were on such good terms, and this will always be a sweet memory throughout the rest of my life, be it long or short, near you or far away!

Your life is broadening. Your horizon is extended by all the possibilities of a great mass of human kind whose monotonous variety is measured by infinity; my vision is circumscribed by the sombre circle where the blue of the sea and the blue of heaven touch without merging. Moving in that perfect circle inscribed by the Creator's hand, and of which I am always the centre, I follow the undulant line of the swell—the only motion I am sure of—and think of you who live in the midst of spiritual unrest where the storms that rage spring from the surge of ideas; and from afar I share your joys—and am ready to share your disappointments, while praying that such may be spared you. Think of me always as your very devoted friend and nephew,

J. CONRAD.

Arrived here yesterday.[4] Leave tomorrow; in London by the end of July.[5] By the end of August hope to be on my way to the Ukraine via Paris. If you are there, till then; if not, on my return. Write in care of Messrs. Barr, Moering, 36 Camomile Street, London, E.C.

43. KAZIMIERÓWKA, 14 SEPTEMBER 1893.

Kazimierówka. 14 Sept., '93.

My dear, good Aunt,

Everything has happened as you suspected regarding my trip to the Ukraine. I found your kind letters (two) in London; and so, not knowing where to find you, though nevertheless sure you were no longer in Paris. I left by the Dutch route, which is the shortest, since, as you well appreciate, I was very anxious to see the best of uncles. I intended to write in time for you to find my letter on arriving in Paris.

I was living here quietly, then, happy to be near my

4. After a voyage of fifty-six days (Galsworthy, "Reminiscences of C," p. 74).

5. Actually, the 26th (*LL*, I, 153).

uncle, whose affection is so steadfast and so dear to me, when I was handed your third letter (via London), the contents of which, to tell you the truth, rather astonished me. It is quite true that Marysieńka[1] is getting married, but what in the name of all folly should I be doing in this marriage business! I can, however, hardly believe you were speaking seriously in your letter, for it must have seemed strange to you that a person would thus dash all of a sudden from the depths of Australia—without warning a soul —to the depths of the Ukraine to throw himself into the arms of— The whole idea is very funny.

Little M. is marrying Mr. Rakowski, son of one of my uncle's neighbors. He was here some days before my arrival to announce the matter officially to my uncle. M. has made a good marriage (or will do so), everything considered, for she was a governess with those worthy folk, who are said to be much taken with her—the entire family.

I see regretfully that you are a little unsettled.[2] It is doubtless only a temporary reaction after the continuous work throughout the winter. Nothing lasts forever. I hope your next letter will speak of new hopes, new enthusiasm, new triumphs. As for myself, I have been quite ill and in bed for five days. It is nice to be ill here (if one must be ill). My uncle has nursed me as if I were a little child. He kisses your hands and always speaks of you with the warmest regard and friendship.

I am going back to London about the end of September without stopping anywhere. I shall probably go through Amsterdam. I am anxious to return and find work, as I have left the "Torrens" for good.[3]

As soon as I get back I shall write you. Meanwhile I embrace you heartily and am ever your affectionate nephew and very faithful friend,

J. CONRAD.

My most dutiful respects to your mother.

1. Mme. P.'s niece by marriage, Marie Ołdakowska. See L. 10 and App. IV (and note *LF*, p. 203, n. 2).

2. The last word is in English.

3. The Certificate of Discharge was issued on 26 July, 1893 (Keating, *C. Mem. Lib.*, p. 401). (Cf. "The 'Torrens': A Personal Tribute," p. 26.)

44. London, 5 November 1893.

5 Nov., '93. 17 Gillingham St.

My dear Aunt,

I hope you will kindly pardon my long silence. I have no excuse to offer, as I am now unemployed and, since my return from Poland, have spent my days in disheartening idleness.[1] You who describe things and men, and so have lifted a corner of the veil, well know there are times when the mind is numb, when months slip by, and when hope itself seems dead. I am going through one of those times. It seems to me I have seen nothing, see nothing, and ever shall see nothing. I could swear that there is nothing but the void outside the walls of the room where I write these lines. Surely this is like the beginning of hopeless imbecility. What do you think? In any case you see I am not even worthy of your anger. Very humbly, ever your most devoted

J. Conrad.

45. London, 26 November 1893.

26 Nov., 1893.

My beloved Aunt,

I am leaving London tomorrow[1] in the English steamship "Adowa," which the Franco-Canadian Company has leased for service between French and Canadian ports. I received my appointment to the berth of second officer[2] this morning quite unexpectedly,[3] and so have hardly time to throw my things together in great haste and dash on board, as my period of service begins tonight at eleven o'clock.

It was full time, for I was beginning to slip into a very black melancholy. Result of idleness.

I am charmed with "Joujou."[4] It is completely and de-

1. C. writes of this idleness in *PR*, pp. 7 f.

---

1. But cf. *LL*, I, 154, where 29 Nov. is given as the date of this departure. This was, too, the date when C. "signed on" (Keating, *C. Mem. Lib.*, p. 400).

2. The two words are in English.

3. This event is described in detail in *PR*, pp. 6–11.

4. This short story by Mme. P. appeared in the *Figaro* ("Supplément littéraire") for 29 July, 1893.

liciously shocking.[5] How the devil did you come on it!? Pardon sailor-language. A hearty embrace. I shall be in a French port the day after tomorrow,[6] from where I shall drop you a line before sailing. I am, as ever and forever, your very devoted nephew,

J. Conrad.

Care of Barr, Moering & Co., 72–73 Fore Street, E.C.

46. Rouen, 6 December 1893.

6 Dec., '93. S.S. "Adowa," Rouen.

Dear Aunt,

Just a line to tell you I am here in France. We expect to leave Saturday[1] for La Rochelle,[2] and from there go to Halifax (North America).[3]

Drop me a line at La Rochelle.

Use this address:

Mr. Conrad, 2d off., S.S. "Adowa,"
La Rochelle,
La Palisse.[4]

I should much like to hear from you before leaving Europe.

My health is pretty good. And yours?!

47. Rouen, 18 December 1893.

18 Dec., 1893. "Adowa," Rouen.

My dear Aunt,

You will be surprised to receive my letter from here, but it seems that the Franco-Canadian Company has not kept to its agreement with our owner, and consequently our sailing has been put off. Just now there is a trial to be held in

5. The last word is in English.
6. The "Adowa" arrived at Rouen on 4 Dec. (*LL,* I, 154).

1. The 9th.
2. But cf. L. 47.
3. The project, which fell through, was to make regular sailings to Canada with French emigrants. See *PR,* pp. 10 f.
4. The adjacent port (La Pallice).

Paris next Friday[1]—a suit for damages—but in any event the affair has fallen through and we shall not go to Canada. As soon as the trial is finished we shall return to England, to load for India, the Persian Gulf, or—I don't know where. Nothing is certain except our ignorance of our future movements.

It seems unnatural to be in France without seeing you! I have had a mind to escape and run off to Paris—even to leave the ship for good—but I have had to give up all these dreams. The fact is that I can't afford this little luxury of affection. And anyhow they wouldn't let me go. So there you are! What can I do? There are no pleasant necessities. They are always harsh—you know, the usual expression. Why? Very funny all the same. Well, I have already had the honor of mentioning in several of my letters that life is wrongside out. I have made this an article of faith and am resigned to it.

Drop me a line here to console me. Do you want to do me a good turn? Yes, of course! Well, you who are acquainted with so many people perhaps know someone in the Administration of the Suez Canal. I should like to find out how one goes about getting a job as Canal pilot. I don't believe it is very hard to do, but yet you have to know how. And if you could learn that, you would also be able to find out how much it pays. I have an idea it is no Eldorado.

Forgive my directness, and ever so many thanks in advance; but remember that the thing is of no importance, and don't bother too much. Always your very devoted

CONRAD.

48. ROUEN, 20 DECEMBER 1893.

20 Dec., 1893. S.S. "Adowa," Rouen.

Dear Aunt,

I have just received your letter. Ever and ever so many thanks for the book you promise me,[1] for your prompt reply, for the kind words of affection you write me.

1. The 22d.

1. Her *Le Mariage du fils Grandsire,* which C. was to receive in Rouen on 6 Jan., 1894 (L. 51).

Why are you angry with the poor Company, which can't help itself? As for me, I forgive it. There is a frightful storm in the Atlantic, and it is better weather in port than out. It is true that life here is not very amusing, but as I am paid to be bored! . . . All the same, this is leading to nothing and I am beginning to feel old. You must be established somewhere if you have any notion of living. But of that, to tell the truth, I don't see the necessity, though on the other hand I am not prepared to take arsenic or jump overboard. So I must get settled.

I am taking steps—or rather they are being taken for me—to get a job in the pearl fisheries off the Australian coast. The idea is a pleasant one, but the matter is far from easy, so that while meditating on the vanity of things here below, and especially of promises, I thought of the Suez. The work is light. One is not too far away, and I suppose one can earn a living at it. I ask no more than that.

I am awaiting the book impatiently. Is it the novel about Lille? Or the story of the madman?[2]

Thanks once again!

A big hug.

Your very devoted nephew,

J. Conrad.

49. Rouen, 25 December 1893.

25 Dec., 1893. "Adowa," Rouen.

My dear Aunt,

It is really too kind of you to go to so much trouble for your worthless nephew. I thank you a million times. I am sending herewith the draft of my service record (No. 1). Will you please correct the mistakes? And as for the letter to the president, I hardly know how to write it. This is my idea; what do you think of it (No. 2)?[1]

I send you at the same time my best wishes for the New

2. It was the novel about Lille, *Le Mariage du fils Grandsire*. The story of the madman was "Simple Récit . . .," an adaptation by her from the Polish of Mme. Sophie Kowerska. It had appeared in *RDM* for 1 Aug., 1889.

1. These two enclosures are missing from the collection.

Year. With us this is only a matter of form, as you must know that not a day of my life (or yours) passes without my wishing you all possible and imaginable happinesses. And there are so few of them! So few! But that's not my fault.

So Justine[2] has promised!!! And I, who was thinking of. . . . Well, let it go! What bad luck I have! There can be no mistake about that!! Life has been a desert since I read your letter. Only the thought of the Canal saves me from suicide. Justine or the Canal; the Canal or Justine. There is nothing beyond.

It is an awful blow that has descended upon you in the shape of the Jonakowskis.[3] What on earth are they doing there? I have an idea, good Aunt! Papa would make a fine coachman, since they are such great lords. Still, you have to be honest to make a career of hack-driving, and the father is, you know, a little . . . shady, according to what I have heard.

I have the honor to inform you that the tribe of savages which has just invaded Paris is very little "cousinly" to me. I don't want those people calling me "charming boy." It is impertinent.

I embrace you heartily with all the gratitude, all the affection, you deserve, and am ever your very devoted nephew and servant,

J. CONRAD.

50. ROUEN, 1 JANUARY 1894.

1 Jan., 1894. Rouen.

Dear Aunt,

Here are my best New Year's wishes. I have purposely waited until the day so as to avoid any mistake. I am thinking of you as this year begins! I am writing this in a dirty little café.[1] We (all of us on board) are so completely strapped that, after vainly having tried to borrow ten sous from all my shipmates, I reached a decision and have just

2. It has not been possible to identify her.

3. Other references to this family, about which we can add nothing, are in App. III, no. 1, and L. 90.

1. Note the similar café in *PR*, p. 5.

assaulted a gentleman (a complete stranger, too) and stolen his purse. He lies sprawled at the corner while I enjoy the fruits of my industry. Doubtless he leaves a widow and several small children—sad, but what could I do? I had to have a stamp for this letter; and what's more, he looked stupid!

I want my book! ! ! ! ! ! ! ! ! ! No, your book! I am waiting for it. I must have it, and as quickly as possible! I don't understand your hesitation. It is probably to set me on edge. You have succeeded............(here an attack of nerves)............

Ah, I feel better. A little glass of cognac has set me up. I can't go see the Bishop.[2] I have no fit clothes, and besides, what good would it do? Do you like that Bishop? From what you have said, I doubt it. Well, no more do I.

I embrace you heartily and am ever your very devoted nephew and servant,

J. CONRAD.

51. ROUEN, 7 JANUARY 1894.

Later than L. 50, for her novelette (*Le Mariage du fils Grandsire*), which she had promised to send to Rouen (L. 48), has not arrived; earlier, also, than L. 52, which was written when C. was about to return to London. The only Sunday between the dates of Lrs. 50 and 52 was 7 Jan.

Sunday. 2 P.M.

My dear Aunt,

(Here is another of my effusions inspired by spirituous liquor sold at retail. But one can tell that by the paper;[1] and also doubtless, there arises from this elegant missive a delicate scent of inebriety. Isn't that so?)

Last evening I escaped from the ship for the pilgrimage to the station. I have my package numbered four thousand and something. Consider for a moment a work of art entitled "Package No. 4000, etc., etc."!! I said to the person at the window: "Sir, your notice of receipt is an outrage."

2. Probably the Bishop also mentioned in L. 7 and App. III, no. 2, whom we have been unable to identify.

1. Cheap, cross-ruled French paper similar to that of Lrs. 50 and 52 (App. V, no. 19).

"Beg pardon?" "An outrage; you are bourgeois rascals. Do you understand?" "No," he replied, "but you're an anarchist, you are! where is your bomb?" Thereupon, while he is crying "Help!" I flee and throw myself into a cab. "Driver," say I, "I'm in a hurry. Unhitch your horse; the cab will go faster." "Splendid idea!" cried he. And that is how I escaped from the police who thirsted for my blood.

It was late. I have read only the first chapter. I cannot, even if I dared to, judge. But with the very first pages I am in the presence of your charming personality. It is really you!

I haven't time to read the book[2] at one sitting, but I shall have the pleasure of tasting it slowly.

Received your card. Ever so many thanks. You write English very nicely.—If you are a good little girl I shall let you read my story of Almayer[3] when I have finished it.

I embrace you heartily.

Your devoted nephew,

J. CONRAD.

52. ROUEN, 9 JANUARY 1894.

9 Jan., 1894.

Dear Aunt,

We leave Rouen tomorrow for London. Write me there in care of Barr, Moering, 72 Fore Street. A hug. Very busy.

Yours,

J. CONRAD.

2. Though C. invariably uses the word *livre* in referring to *Le Mariage du fils Grandsire,* we know that on another occasion he uses this word when referring to a work then appearing in serial form. See L. 83, n. 2. In the present instance, however, what he probably received was an actual book. See L. 76. If so, this would appear to have been an advance copy. *Le Mariage du fils Grandsire* was published in book form by Hachette early in 1894 after evidently having appeared in the *Mode pratique,* a weekly magazine launched by Hachette in Dec., 1891. See Lorentowicz and Chmurski, *La Pologne en France,* nos. 2874 f., which we have modified in the light of the *Bibliographie de la France* for 1892 and 1894, having been unable to examine the *Mode pratique.*

3. *AF* was begun in the autumn of 1889 (*PR,* pp. 13 and 73 f.; *Lib. of John Quinn,* Pt. 1, p. 165) and finished, except for some revision (Lrs. 60 f.), on 24 Apr., 1894 (L. 59). C. commenced writing the tenth of its twelve chapters aboard the "Adowa" at Rouen (*PR,* p. 1).

53. London, 20 January 1894.

[*Engraved letterhead:* The British and Foreign Transit Agency. Barr, Moering & Co. Offices, 72 & 73, Fore Street, London E.C.]

20 Jan., [189]4.

My dear Aunt,

On arriving in London[1] I found your letter, for which I thank you ever and ever so much.—You are right. Poles are lazy. I must say I don't quite know how I could help you.[2] I have no news from Poland. My uncle and I correspond once or twice a month. Family news, etc., etc.

I am reading *Le fils Grandsire* with delight. It is charming, characteristic, alive. I shall finish the book tomorrow and speak of it in my next letter.—I am very much put out at having to leave the "Adowa."[3] It was so convenient being employed near Europe. I rather fear that I shall be forced to go on a long voyage very shortly.

Don't let yourself become stultified! You speak of this with a levity that scandalizes me. It's a serious thing, you know. Nothing easier than to get rusty.—Tell me, are you absolutely omniscient? Whence comes this knowledge of bric-a-brac, of old books and old pictures?

Until soon (on paper).

Your very devoted

J. Conrad.

54. London, 2 February 1894.

2 Feb., 1894. 17 Gillingham St., London, S.W.

Dear Aunt,

I finished the book some while ago, then reread several passages in anticipation of the time when I can reread it entirely.

My appreciation of your book, of any book, is purely emotional. Of the workmanship, labor, carving—if I may

1. According to Jean-Aubry, on 12 Jan. (*LL,* I, 155).

2. With, perhaps, some of the details in her forthcoming *Marylka.* See Lrs. 60 ff.

3. In the Certificate of Discharge (facsimile in Keating, *C. Mem. Lib.*, p. 400), the discharge proper is dated 17 Jan.

so express myself—I can hardly judge; and as emotion is a personal matter my judgment can only be incomplete and very often wrong. And so you see I miss the joy of "one who knows," of one who views a work of art in its entirety. But I am at liberty, fortunately, to lose myself in the contemplation of lovely images, to listen to the music of written words, to live the life, to breathe the air, to experience the joys and sorrows, the hopes and regrets, that fill this corner of the world your magician's pen has created. And it is very much alive, your little corner of the world, with its silent tumult of passions and its final cry of anguish. The true cry, that—which is only a murmur of the soul that has become exhausted in its struggle towards the Promised Land.

The dominant note of the work is its sad charm, but the details brought joy to me. What a series of charming pictures! The return of the Clochases; the journey to the cemetery, with the young girl draping herself in a veil light and fragile as her dream of happiness; the scene with Rose. But why enumerate? I should have to recite the whole book.

And the master-touches! There are some which simply delighted me. Aunt Colombe eating her tunny-fish by candlelight. I positively love Aunt C. And Mme. Frandhre, and Catherine, and the diplomatic old junk-dealer. I love them all. While reading certain passages I clapped as one applauds at the theatre. And how many likeable characters you have succeeded in portraying! Indeed, there is not one who is not likeable in his own way, for they are all so alive, and so completely human!

If I have misunderstood or fallen short in appreciation, you must not hold it too much against me. It is better to be hard of hearing than deaf, and to see dimly than not at all. The creator knows his creatures. We others raise a corner of the veil and look upon the beings of your imagination through the mist of our faults, of our disappointments, and of our regrets. One may be permitted to make a mistake when there are so many who close their eyes and stop their ears! Your devoted

J. CONRAD.

55. London, 18 February 1894.

18 Feb., '94. 17 Gillingham St.

My dear Aunt,

I have just received a message from Poland. My uncle died the 11th[1] of this month, and it seems as if everything has died in me, as if he has carried away my soul with him.

I had been ill for some days and was beginning to recover a little when I received this news.[2] I embrace you heartily.

J. Conrad.

56. London, 2 March 1894.

2 Mar., 1894. 17 Gillingham St.

My dear Aunt,

I am very sorry to hear you are ill, and with neuralgia of all things! I know something of it[1] and can therefore sympathize with you understandingly.

I am a little like a wild animal; I try to hide myself when I am suffering in body or mind, and right now I am suffering in both.

The worst of it is that in the idleness to which I am now condemned I can hardly forget my suffering. Forgetfulness is sweet, but difficult to find.

If possible I shall come to Brussels for a little visit,[2] but I don't know whether I shall be able to. It is not that I don't want to. I am trying to find employment and I dare not leave London just now for fear of missing an opportunity.

Do you think an answer will be forthcoming to my application for employment on the Suez? Even if it is only a re-

1. The 10th would appear to be more accurate, for *Polski słownik biog.*, II, 163, gives 29 Jan. as the date, and the difference at this time between the Russian and Gregorian calendars was twelve days.

2. According to Jean-Aubry, C. heard by telegram of his uncle's death the day it occurred (*LL*, I, 157). The opening words of the letter, then, are evidently to be interpreted broadly. Cf. Lrs. 9, introd.; 23 ("just this moment"); and 35, n. 1.

---

1. For instance, in Feb., 1891. See L. 14.

2. He evidently did so during this month. See L. 57, n. 2.

fusal? Or must I take the silence as a refusal? I should much like to know your opinion about this.

Thanks for your good words. You cannot know how precious your affection is to me! I embrace you heartily. Your devoted friend and nephew,

J. CONRAD.

57. LONDON, 29 MARCH OR 5 APRIL (?) 1894.

Mentioning Chap. XI (of *AF*) as in process of completion, this letter precedes L. 58 (dated 16 Apr., 1894), in which Chap. XI is spoken of as completed. And because the present letter was written from London, the Thursday of the heading cannot be later than 5 Apr., since C. was at Elstree for a period of ten days (L. 61) ending on 20 Apr. (see the "I return there [to London] next Friday" of L. 58). But it can likewise hardly be as much as two weeks earlier than 5 Apr., since a considerable interval, during which C. appears to have visited Brussels (see n. 2), must have separated the present letter from L. 56. Probably, then, the Thursday of the heading was either 29 Mar. or 5 Apr.

Thursday. London. 17 Gillingham St., S.W.

My dearest Aunt,

Forgive me for not having written sooner, but I am in the midst of struggling with Chap. XI; a struggle to the death, you know! If I let up, I am lost! I am writing you just before going out. I must go out sometimes, alas! I begrudge each minute I spend away from paper. I do not say "from pen," because I write very little, but inspiration comes to me in looking at the paper. Then there are soaring flights; my thought goes wandering through vast spaces filled with shadowy forms. All is yet chaos, but, slowly, the apparitions change into living flesh, the shimmering mists take shape, and—who knows?—something may be born of the clash of nebulous ideas.

I send you the first page[1] (of which I have made a copy) to give you an idea of the appearance of my manuscript. I

1. This page, containing numerous alterations of various kinds, was in the collection when it was acquired by Mr. Keating and is now in the possession of Dr. A. S. W. Rosenbach.

Almayer's Folly

Chapter XI No 1.

He turned over with an impatient sigh, and pillowing his head on his bent arm lay quietly with his face to the dying fire. The glowing embers shone redly in a small circle putting a gleam into his wide open eyes, and at every deep breath the fine white ash of bygone fires rose in a light cloud from before his parted lips and danced away from the warm glow to lose itself in the moonbeams pouring upon Bulangi's clearing. — In the shadowless square of light shining on a smooth and level expanse of young rice-shoots the fire and the man, the small shelter-house rising on two high posts above him and a pile of brushwood near by, seemed very small and as if lost in the great flood of tender green iridescence reflected from the ground. — On three sides of the clearing — appearing very far away in the deceptive light — the big trees of the forest lashed together [illegible] with manifold bonds by tangled creepers looked down upon the growing life at their feet with the sombre resignation of captive giants that had lost faith

MANUSCRIPT PAGE OF *ALMAYER'S FOLLY*

This page, here considerably reduced, is the one mentioned in Letter 57

owe you this since I have seen yours.[2] I like, so I do, to conform to the rules of etiquette.

I embrace you heartily. Ever yours,

J. CONRAD.

Send me the address at Lille.[3]

58. ELSTREE, HERTS., 16 APRIL 1894.

[*Embossed letterhead:* Elstree, Herts.]

16 Apr., '94.

Dear Aunt,

Just a word to tell you that I am at the Sandersons',[1] that my health is so-so, and that Chapter XI is finished. Nine thousand words—longer but much worse than the others. I am beginning Chapter XII in a quarter of an hour.

Please let me know how you are and how your work[2] is progressing. I hope your characters are well and follow in the path where their destiny and your pen lead them. A brief note to my address in London, if you please. I return there next Friday.[3]

I embrace you heartily.

Your very devoted nephew,

J. CONRAD.

59. LONDON, 24 APRIL 1894.

C. had evidently returned to London before this letter was written. See L. 58.

24 Apr., 1894. 11 A.M.

My dear Aunt,

It is my sorrowful duty to inform you of the death of Mr.

2. This is one of several indications that he had probably made a recent visit to Brussels (see esp. Lrs. 56, 60, and 63), bringing with him a typewritten copy of Chaps. I–X of *AF* (see Lrs. 51 and 59 ff.).

3. Probably the same address ("Rue de la Barre") that is mentioned in L. 19.

---

1. C. had met Edward Lancelot Sanderson when the latter was a passenger on board the "Torrens." *An Outcast of the Islands* (1896) was dedicated to him and *The Mirror of the Sea* (1906) to his mother. He succeeded his father as headmaster of the Elstree Preparatory School. See Marrot, *Life and Letters of Galsworthy*, pp. 73–89, and *LL*, II, 123.

2. *Marylka.* See Lrs. 60 ff.

3. The 20th.

Kaspar Almayer, which occurred this morning at three o'clock.

It's finished! A scratch of the pen writing "The End,"[1] and suddenly that whole company of people who have spoken in my ear, moved before my eyes, lived with me for so many years, becomes a troop of phantoms, who are withdrawing, growing dim, and merging—indistinct and pallid—with the sunlight of this brilliant and sombre day.

Since awakening this morning it seems to me that I have buried a part of myself in the pages lying here before my eyes. And yet I am happy—a little.

I shall send you the two chapters[2] as soon as they are typed.

Thanks for your letter.[3]

I embrace you heartily.

Ever your faithful and devoted

J. Conrad.

60. London, Late April (?) 1894.

Hastily scribbled on a scrap of paper, this note pertains almost wholly to Pts. XIX and XX of Mme. P.'s *Marylka,* a novelette of twenty-four short parts first published in *RDM* for 15 Feb. and 1 and 15 Mar., 1895. It had, however, been submitted for publication and "read" before 12 July, 1894 (L. 64). Hence this note, which unmistakably deals with the initial planning of these parts rather than with their final revision, must have been written some weeks prior to this date. The last sentence, on the other hand, refers to the revision of *AF,* a labor which, likewise mentioned in L. 61, must have been undertaken after 24 Apr., when the first complete text of the novel was finished (L. 59).

For placing this note before L. 61, the following reasons, all of which lack finality, may be advanced: (1) less detailed and restricted than the reference in L. 61 to the revision of the first chapters, the last sentence of the note appears to be the earlier of these references; (2) it is natural to suppose that the words, "Happy that you are working," occurred in the first of the group of letters of this period to discuss the literary problems now confronting her; (3) of these problems, those discussed in the note would, in the ordinary course of things, precede both the problem (treated

1. This, with "April, 1894" beneath it, occurs on the last page of the autograph MS. (*Lib. of John Quinn,* Pt. 1, p. 164). The French reads, *le mot de la fin.*

2. XI and XII (Lrs. 61–63). Only XI was sent (see Lrs. 72 ff.).

3. Probably in answer to L. 57 but not forwarded to Elstree.

in Lrs. 61 f.) of deciding upon an apt name for one of the characters, and the problem (treated in L. 62) of finding a satisfactory title for the complete work; (4) Lrs. 61–64 are apparently too closely linked to permit of the intrusion of this note and the postcard it answers; (5) this postcard, discussing *Marylka,* may well have been the "brief note" requested in L. 58 (see L. 59, n. 3).

It may further be suggested that this present note, which alone in the entire series lacks any heading whatever, perhaps accompanied the typescript of Chap. XI of *AF* when it was sent to Mme. P. Since C. had promised in L. 59 to send Chaps. XI and XII, and since in L. 61 he wrote that he would shortly send Chap. XII, Chap. XI must have gone to her either with L. 61 or between the dates of these two letters.

Received your postcard.[1]

The only procedure is to submit one's resignation to the War Office. One can get away. Generally, one requests leave upon resigning. Then one goes. Once granted, a resignation cannot be withdrawn, or it is at least very difficult, I believe. We decided[2] on Brześć, but Zamość (a fortress) is not far either. The idea of placing Lia in a *szynk* is good. The meeting is possible there—more so there than elsewhere.[3] Happy that you are working. As for me, I am rewriting the first four chapters.[4]

Yours,

J. C.

61. London, 2 May 1894.

2 May, '94. London. 17 Gillingham St.

Dear Aunt,

I have just received your letter. A good letter that gives

1. The last word is in English.

2. Evidently during the recent visit he appears to have made to Brussels. See L. 57, n. 2.

3. The preceding details concern *Marylka,* Pts. XIX and XX, which were published in *RDM* for 15 Mar., 1895, pp. 438–443. Thadée Radowski, in order to marry Marylka Bielska, the daughter of a Polish patriot, takes steps to resign as an officer of dragoons in the Russian army. When she subsequently refuses him, he is able to retain his commission. At Zamość, near his station, he had begun an affair with Lia, a young Jewess, their first meeting having occurred in an alehouse (*szynk*). Brześć (Brest-Litovsk) and Zamość are fortified towns in the general vicinity of Lublin.

4. Mr. J. D. Gordan (see *infra,* Bibliography) has made an illuminating study of this revision as revealed in the manuscript and the typescript. Among other things, the dominant motif of paternal love, which was not in C.'s mind when he began, is studiously worked into the opening pages.

me much pleasure, a letter that makes me want to be near you. Do you understand? Thanks! It is so gratifying to be entirely understood, and you have understood me from start to finish.

If you insist, let it be "Wojtek."[1] Only don't forget that "Wojtek" is a diminutive; and, if your Wojtek is a grave and serious man, mightn't the name be at odds with the character? But so long as you *see* the character as "Wojtek," it is impossible to change the name. I fully understand that.

My health is not exceptional. I spent ten days[2] at the Sandersons' in Elstree and it did me good. The air is excellent there.—I find the work of revising my first three chapters not only unpleasant but absolutely painful. And hard besides! And yet it must be done!

I shall soon send you the last chapter.[3] It begins with a *trio*—Nina, Dain, Almayer—and ends with a long *solo* for Almayer which is almost as long as Tristan's in Wagner. However, you will see! But I am much afraid you will find the thing insipid.

I embrace you heartily.

Your very devoted

J. Conrad.

62. London, 17 May(?) 1894.

The *"Let it be 'Wojtek'!"* places this letter with, and, we may suppose, immediately subsequent to, L. 61. The references to *AF* in the two letters lend support to this ordering, for whereas C. informed Mme. P. in L. 61 that he would soon send Chap. XII, he now gives his reason for not having done so. As for the remarks pertaining to Mme. P.'s *Marylka,* they indicate a period in the progress of that work several weeks earlier than 12 July, when C. wrote to congratulate her upon its having pleased the "reader" (L. 64). Hence all the facts point to a date somewhat later than that of L. 61. In the light of the opening sentence and the heading, 17 May appears to be most likely.

Thursday.

My dear, good Aunt,

Forgive the tardiness of my reply. I have been very

1. Woytek Radowski, the hero of *Marylka.*
2. In the middle of April. See L. 57, introd.
3. But see Lrs. 62 f. and 72. See also the last paragraph in L. 60, introd.

busy,[1] and also I thought I would be able to give you good news of myself today. I was almost sure, though I am hardly an optimist, of obtaining the command of a ship. Well, it fell through. Instead of sending you word, as I had intended, of the achievement of my desire, I send you a sigh of regret and a growl of anger. However, it can't be helped! I am beginning to get used to disappointments of this sort.

Why do you say "my miserable novel"! I am sure it will be a fine thing. It happens that I reread *Yaga* just the other day. It gave me intense pleasure. I read slowly and mingled my dreams with those pages I love so well.

Forgive me for not sending you my Chap. XII. The whole manuscript is in the hands of quite a distinguished critic: Edmund Gosse.[2] I have no idea how long he will keep it. But as you are now busy with your own work I would as soon not interrupt you.

The question of the title is important. What you say is perfectly true. "Cœur de jeune fille" is good but rather long, don't you think? Couldn't you find something shorter? A term expressing, for example, some emotion or other; "a state of soul," as your letter has it.

Let it be "Wojtek"!

I embrace you warmly. I write no more, for my heart is rather heavy with disappointment and I don't want to "jeremiadize."

Another letter will follow shortly. Ever yours,

J. CONRAD.

1. How long he continued to revise *AF* is unknown. On the wrapper of the autograph MS., C. wrote: "Finished on the 22 May 1894" (*Lib. of John Quinn*, Pt. 1, p. 165). But because the dates that follow this statement are wrong, little reliance can be put on it.

2. We are unable to throw much light on this interesting fact, of which there appears to be no further record. During the early 1890's Gosse edited for the firm of William Heinemann the "International Library," a series of foreign novels translated into English (Whyte, *Heinemann*, pp. 61–68), and it may be that *AF*, written by a Pole, was considered for this series. More probably, however, the MS. was submitted to him for his personal advice. His biographer, the Hon. Evan Charteris, K.C. (to whom we are kindly indebted for some correspondence on this reference), comments on Gosse's interest at this period in writers not yet established (*Life and Letters of Gosse*, pp. 234–239). He writes, also: "No appeal to Gosse could be made in vain. He was an unrivalled counsellor in literary matters; he would take endless pains to give advice and encouragement. He was out to help" (p. 236).

63. London, June(?) 1894.

Evidently this letter immediately precedes L. 64 (dated 12 July, 1894), for L. 64 appears to be in reply to a letter in which Mme. P. answered the questions here asked concerning her presence in Paris, her novel, and her health. And, if this conclusion is correct, the present letter was probably written earlier than 4 July, when C. submitted *AF* to T. Fisher Unwin & Co. (L. 64, n. 1), for otherwise he would probably have informed her of this fact here. The "long silence," also, would place it considerably later than L. 62. Since L. 62 may be tentatively assigned to the middle of May, the present letter probably belongs in June (Wednesdays on the 6th, etc.).

Wednesday. London. 17 Gillingham St.

Dear Aunt,

Are you in Paris? If you send me word I shall forward the twelfth and last chapter, which is ready. How is your novel getting along? I am worried. At least you are not ill?! I realize that my long silence is infamous treatment of the best of Aunts, but you know that I have a natural aptitude for crime. Moreover, it is the office of the good to forgive the wicked. I hasten to say that you belong in the first category.

I am neither ill nor well—though more nearly ill than well. I spend my time as best I can while waiting for regular employment. And I am neither more nor less stupid than in Brussels when I had the pleasure of inflicting myself on you.[1] If you haven't time to write, please send me the word "Paris" on a postcard.

I embrace you heartily. Your very devoted

J. Conrad.

64. London, 12 July 1894.

12 July, '94.

My dear Aunt,

I am happy to know that your novel pleased the publishers' reader. Yet I had no fear on that score, and am much more happy to know that you are well in body and mind.

As for me, I am well in neither the one nor the other. I

1. For the probable time of this visit, see L. 57, n. 2.

sent my manuscript to Fisher Unwin & Co.,[1] who publish a series of anonymous novels.[2] No reply yet. It will doubtless come in the form of a return of that masterpiece, in anticipation of which I enclosed the necessary stamps.

To tell you the truth, I feel no interest in what happens to "Almayer's Folly." That's finished. And in any case its fate could be no more than an inconsequential episode in my life.

Yes, it would be good to see each other again! But! . . . In the meanwhile it is pleasant to think of your true and tender friendship. That sweetens many things. I kiss your hands. Your friend and very affectionate nephew,

J. C. KORZENIOWSKI.

I am sending this to Passy,[3] though you are no longer in Paris.[4] I have no other address.

65. LONDON, 20 JULY (?) 1894.

Pen, ink, and handwriting place this and L. 66 in 1894. The paper, also, is of the same make (though not watermarked with the same year) as Lrs. 68–70 and 72 (App. V, nos. 24 f.). The handwriting resembles that of L. 64 very closely, and there is probably a link between the postscript of that letter and the opening paragraph of this one. Both the present letter and L. 66 reflect, too, the physical condition he describes in Lrs. 67 f. Hence we may suppose that this letter was written during the latter part of July, and probably, since Lrs. 66 f. were evidently written between it and L. 68 (dated 8 Aug., 1894), on Friday, 20 July.

Friday.

My dear, good Aunt,

I received your letter this morning. As you wrote me you were leaving Paris for some time, I refrained from writing until further word came.

So you are in a period of "dark gloom"! I well understand this regret for the past as it slips away little by little,

1. On 4 July. This we know from C.'s letter to Unwin of 8 Sept. See L. 72, n. 1. The firm was located at 11 Paternoster Buildings, E.C. (*LL*, I, 183).
2. Unwin's "Pseudonym Library." See L. 70, n. 1.
3. Her permanent residence. See L. 24, n. 2.
4. She was evidently visiting in Brussels and Lille. See Lrs. 68 f.

leaving traces of its passage in tombs and regrets. It is only this that is eternal.

Remember, though, that one is never entirely alone. Why are you afraid? And of what? Is it of solitude or of death? O strange fear! The only two things that make life bearable! But cast fear aside. Solitude never comes—and death must often be waited for during long years of bitterness and anger. Do you prefer that?

But you are afraid of yourself; of the inseparable being forever at your side—master and slave, victim and executioner—who suffers and causes suffering. That's how it is! One must drag the ball and chain of one's selfhood to the end. It is the [price][1] one pays for the devilish and divine privilege of thought; so that in this life it is only the elect who are convicts[2]—a glorious band which comprehends and groans but which treads the earth amidst a multitude of phantoms with maniacal gestures, with idiotic grimaces. Which would you be: idiot or convict?

I embrace you with all my heart.

J. CONRAD.

66. LONDON, 25 JULY (?) 1894.

See L. 65, introd. The present letter was probably written shortly after L. 65, to which it seems to refer in its opening and closing parts.

Wednesday.

My dear Aunt,

Doubtless you have received my letter and think me crazy. I am so, very nearly. My nervous disorder torments me, makes me miserable, and paralyzes action, thought, everything! I wonder why I exist? It is a frightful condition. Even in the intervals, when I am supposed to be well, I live in fear of the return of this distressing ailment. In the Arab expression applied to those who have incurred the sovereign's wrath, "I live in the shadow of the sword," and I wonder night and morning whether it will fall today, or tomorrow, or the next day.

1. Beginning a new page, C. has omitted the word *prix*.
2. Cf. his remarks about convicts in Lrs. 29 f.

I no longer have the courage to do anything. I have hardly enough to write you. It is an effort, a frenzied dash to finish before the pen falls from my hand with the collapse of utter discouragement. That's how it is! So you see that you are not the only victim of the incomprehensible. I am sorry to have told you all that. Never have I told so much to anyone. You will do well to forget what you have just read.

I am ever yours,

J. CONRAD.

67. LONDON, 30(?) JULY 1894.

Later than L. 64, in which C. wrote that T. Fisher Unwin & Co. had the MS. of *AF*. Earlier, also, than L. 68, which was written when C. was at Champel. And since Monday, 6 Aug., is out of the question, because this date is too close to that of L. 68, it must belong to July. Evidently, too, it follows Lrs. 65 and 66, which appear to have been written during the illness here mentioned. If the dates proposed for them are correct, it must be assigned to 30 July.

Monday. 17 Gillingham St., London, S.W.

Dear Aunt,

I am answering by return post to congratulate you, to tell you how happy I am over your success![1] I have just got up. I have been in bed ten days—ten centuries! I am still ill. How monotonous it is!

I have had no reply from Fisher Unwin. This may go on for months, and in the end I don't think they will accept it. Here in this country, where four novels are published every week (and, good heavens, what novels!), you must dance attendance for a very long time. I think, too, that it is time wasted.

If you have said nothing to the *Revue*, we might perhaps publish "Almayer" not as a translation but as a collaboration. Haven't I a nerve to suggest this to you, dear master! One would think I still had the fever.

I have done nothing, undertaken nothing, tried nothing,

1. This probably refers to the formal acceptance of *Marylka* for publication in *RDM*. See L. 64.

risked nothing, and so have nothing—except the fever. And even that went yesterday, leaving me very weak and depressed. That is my report.

Write me often. I embrace you heartily.

Yours,

J. CONRAD.

Impossible to do anything for the young man.[2] I have asked everyone I know. It's no use! There are already too many young Frenchmen!

68. CHAMPEL, 8 AUGUST 1894.

8 Aug., '94. Champel, near Geneva.

Dear Aunt,

I am taking the waters here and feel no better for it. I left London so suddenly that I had no time to write you. Besides, I have nothing to tell you. My health is not good and my morale is gently ebbing away. What can you expect? It gets tiresome after a while!

Drop me a line from Lille to tell me you are well. I think I shall stay here until the end of the month.[1]

I embrace you. Your very faithful nephew,

J. CONRAD.

La Roseraie,
Champel, Geneva.

69. CHAMPEL, 16(?) AUGUST 1894.

The reference to Expositions indicates 1894 (see n. 1); the postscript, Champel. The paper, too, is that of Lrs. 68, 70, and 72 (App. V, no. 25). The postscript likewise indicates that he is answering her first letter addressed to him at Champel during this period, a letter she wrote in reply to L. 68. Hence the Thursday appears to be 16 Aug. See also L. 70, introd.

Thursday.

Dear Aunt,

I have just received your letter. Very happy that you

2. Perhaps Jean Gachet.

1. Actually, until 6 Sept. See L. 71.

have refused.[1] Your health before everything. And I am also afraid it wouldn't have turned out very well. If you had written the truth, they would have scalped you back there. You know I have little confidence in my compatriots, and especially those of Galicia! It is all for the best. Stay quietly in Lille and Brussels. That is better than chasing about to rather farcical Expositions.

Yet I am glad they made you this offer. This at least shows that they appreciate your talent and your sympathy. They did very well to invite you; you did very well to refuse.[2] But be kind and flatter the poor creatures a little. You know how quick they are to swallow anything. Isn't that so?

A warm embrace. Letter the day after tomorrow.

Your devoted

J. CONRAD.
4 P.M.

Please write to *J. Conrad, Esq.;* I am known only by that name here.

70. CHAMPEL, 18(?) AUGUST 1894.

This letter is apparently the one promised "the day after tomorrow" in L. 69. To assign it to 11 Aug. would be to place it closer to L. 68 than its remarks as to his improved health and renewed literary activity warrant; and 25 Aug. is also unlikely in view of his statement, "I am going back to England the end of August," for had the end of the month been less than a week off he would probably have given the time of his departure in more precise terms. Hence the probable date is 18 Aug.

Saturday. La Roseraie, Champel, Geneva.

Dear Aunt,

Since you have been kind enough to concern yourself in the matter, let's speak of that silly Almayer. I have written asking the return of my MS., and as soon as I get back to England it will await your disposition. I should like to keep

1. To attend and describe the Exposition of Polish art and industry held at Lemberg (Llów) in 1894. See Brandes, *Poland*, p. 112.

2. See, however, L. 91, in which C. remarks, perhaps facetiously, that he wonders whether she had ultimately refused this invitation.

the name "Kamudi"[1] (which is pronounced "Kamondi"), a Malay word meaning "rudder." I don't want any big letters or anything of that sort. How altogether typical of your kindness to think of such things! To have the use of your beautiful language to express my poor thoughts is a joy and an honor. This is not mere politeness, but sincere conviction. The name "Kamondi" in small letters somewhere will suffice. Let your name appear on the title-page—an explanatory note saying that K. collaborated will be enough. Will you do that? But it seems very odd to be writing you all this. I can hardly believe my good luck.

You offer to help me in Brussels with Pécher or the others. I tell you frankly that my reserves are about exhausted and that I must find a position very quickly; so if you are able to do something without too much trouble, I gratefully accept your assistance. With you I have no pride, no false shame, nor any other feelings but those of affection, of trust, and of gratitude. If one must put up money for a command, I can deposit 12,000 francs *the first of March, 1895,* BUT NOT BEFORE.[2] I am ready to take an examination in Belgium if that is necessary. Don't bother too much, though. I too am looking about and am sure of finding something more or less good. Rather *less* than more, it is true, but surely something!

I am reading Maupassant with delight. I have just finished *Le Lys rouge*[3] by Anatole France. It means nothing at all to me. I can do no serious reading. I have begun to write, but only the day before yesterday. I want to make this thing very short—say twenty to twenty-five pages like those of the *Revue.* I am calling it "Two Vagabonds,"[4] and

1. This word, as Mr. J. D. Gordan has informed us, appears on the title-page of the typescript of *AF* (in the possession of Mr. W. B. Leeds) and was the pseudonym adopted by C. when he submitted the novel for publication in T. Fisher Unwin & Co.'s "Pseudonym Library." See L. 64; *LL,* I, 159; *The Journal of Arnold Bennett,* II, 3 f.; and, for a brief description of this series, F. M. Ford, *Return to Yesterday,* p. 131. *AF* was much too long for inclusion in it (see *LL,* I, 159).

2. C.'s possession of this sum undoubtedly awaited the execution of his uncle's will. See *LL,* I, 116.

3. 1894 (Calmann-Lévy, Paris). C.'s copy was of the twenty-seventh edition (*LL,* II, 227).

4. This projected novelette grew into *An Outcast of the Islands* (1896). See L. 81.

I want to sketch in broad outline, without shading or detail, two human wrecks such as one meets in the forsaken corners of the world. A white man and a Malay. You see that I can't get away from Malays. I am devoted to Borneo. What bothers me most is that my figures are so real. I know them so well that they fetter my imagination. The white man is a friend of Almayer; the Malay is our old friend Babalatchi[5] before he arrived at the estate of prime minister and confidential adviser to the Rajah. There it is. But I have no dramatic climax. My head is empty and there is difficulty even in beginning! I shall tell you no more than this! I should like to give it up already.—Do you think that one can make a thing interesting without a woman in it?!

I am going back to England the end of August. I must seriously set about finding work. My health is returning, and as I obviously can't die I must concern myself with living, which is very tiresome. (This is not a pose; I really feel this way!) Write me if you have time to answer this letter. I shall give you notice of my departure. Send me news of your health. You seem to hint that it is not altogether satisfactory, which makes me uneasy.

I embrace you heartily.

Ever yours,

J. CONRAD.

71. CHAMPEL, 5 SEPTEMBER 1894.

[*Printed letterhead:* Champel-les-Bains près Genève, Société anonyme de Champel-Beau-Séjour (Hôtels Beau-Séjour et la Roseraie)]

5 Sept., '94.

Dear Aunt,

I am leaving Champel tomorrow to go direct to London. From there I shall write you in Brussels. I am almost entirely well. Must hope it will last.—Let me have news of you at 17 Gillingham Street, London.

A hearty embrace.

J. CONRAD.

5. He also figures prominently in *AF*.

72. London, 8 September 1894.

8 Sept., 1894. 17 Gillingham St., S.W.

Dear Aunt,

Thanks for your letter in English. You write very well indeed!

I have been here for some days. I feel fairly well and am looking for a suitable position. The two vagabonds are inactive. I am not satisfied with myself—not at all. I lack ideas. I have burnt a great deal. It's all to begin over!

I have just written Fisher Unwin about "Almayer."[1] I am demanding a reply or the return of the MS. When I get it back I will send you the last chapter, which you have not yet read. If I leave, the MS. will be held for you at Messrs. Barr, Moering & Co., 72 & 73 Fore Street, E.C. When you feel the desire to begin, you are to write that it be sent to you. When does your novel start in the *Revue?*[2] I am anxious to read it!

Your idea for the novel about the pilgrimage[3] is excellent! But isn't it a little too soon after *Lourdes?*[4] It will be said you are following the fashion. A year from now I don't think this will be so. I am sure you will make something fine of it. Don't forget that with us religion and patriotism are closely akin. You can turn this complex sentiment to good account. Let me have news of you. A hearty embrace.

Your devoted

J. Conrad.

73. London, 2 October 1894.

[*Engraved letterhead:* The British and Foreign Transit Agency. Barr, Moering & Co. Offices, 72 & 73, Fore Street, London E.C.]

2 Oct., [189]4.

Dear Aunt,

I received your card yesterday. Ever so many thanks for

1. This letter was printed in the *Sat. Rev. of Lit.* (N.Y.), Vol. X, no. 5 (19 Aug., 1933), p. 55.
2. *Marylka* appeared in *RDM* early in 1895. See L. 60, introd.
3. Evidently *Pour Noémi,* though this, her next published novel (see L. 94, n. 2), has only briefly to do with a pilgrimage.
4. By Zola (Charpentier-Fasquelle, Paris, 1894).

TELEGRAMS,
TRANSITUS, LONDON.

AND AT
DYERS HALL WHARF
95, UPPER THAMES STREET.
E.C.

SHIPPING & CUSTOM HOUSE
AGENTS

CONTINENTAL THROUGH TRAFFICS
VIA
FLUSHING, ROTTERDAM, BOULOGNE, &c.

The British and Foreign Transit Agency.

Barr, Moering & Co.

Offices, 72 & 73, Fore Street.

London 2 Octbre 1894
E.C.

Chère Tante.

J'ai reçu Votre carte hier. Je Vous remercie mille fois de penser a moi. Je suis assez occupé avec les négociations pour divers navires. Rien n'a abouti jusqu'apresent. Je ne peu pas obtenir mon manuscript. J'ai réclamé deux fois et chaque foi j'ai eu la reponse que l'on s'en occupe. Je vais attendre quelque jours encore avant de demander le renvoi quand même.

Je vous embrasse de tout mon cœur

J Conrad.

très pressé aujourd'hui. Ecrirai bientot

Letter 73

thinking of me. I am rather busy with negotiations for several ships. Nothing has gone through as yet.

I cannot obtain my manuscript. I have applied twice and each time received the reply that they had it under consideration. I shall wait a few days more before insisting on its return in any event.

A hearty embrace.

J. CONRAD.

Very rushed today. Will write soon.

74. LONDON, 4 OCTOBER 1894.

4 Oct., '94.

My dear Aunt,

My manuscript has been accepted. I have just had the news. F. U. offers me only £20 for the copyright. I have written agreeing to the terms. As he will possess *all* the rights in the work, we shall have to see about your translation. I am much afraid that F. U. will set too high a price. I shall try to reserve the French copyright if I can. That will be a matter to discuss when I see the manager of the firm.

I have taken what was offered, for really the mere fact of publication is very important. Every week dozens of novels come out, and it is terribly difficult to get one's work printed.—Now I need only a ship to be almost happy.

My health is pretty good. I have had a frightful cold for two days, and right now my head is bursting. You will forgive the incoherence of this letter. The publisher also told me that if I had something shorter (25,000 words)[1] he would like to see it. It is quite flattering. I have nothing. The two vagabonds are idle. I am too busy running after ships. Nothing yet in that direction.

A hearty embrace. Ever your devoted and faithful

J. CONRAD.

1. *AF* ran to almost 65,000 words.

75. London, 10 October 1894.

10 Oct., '94.

Dearest and best of Aunts,

Thanks for your card. Victory! I have the French copyright for myself alone. Let me tell you of my interview.[1]

At first the two "readers"[2] of the firm received me and complimented me effusively (were they by any chance making fun of me?). Then I was conducted into the head's presence to talk business. He told me frankly that if I wanted to assume part of the risk of publication I could have a share of the profits. Otherwise I get £20 and the French rights. I chose the second alternative. "We are paying you very little," he said; "but consider, my dear Sir, that you are an unknown and that your book appeals to a very limited public. Then there is the question of taste. Will the public like it? We too are running something of a risk. We shall bring you out in a handsome volume at six shillings, and you know that what we publish always gets serious attention in the literary journals. You may be sure of a long notice in the *Saturday Review* and the *Athenæum,* not to mention the general press. That is why we are thinking of not publishing you until April of next year, in the season. We shall start printing the work at once so that you may read the proof, and we shall send the proof-sheets[3] to Mme. Poradowska before Christmas. Write something shorter, of the same kind, for our 'Pseudonym Library,' and if it suits us we shall be very happy to give you a much better cheque."

There you are. I am proceeding very gingerly with a vagabond under each arm in the hope of selling them to Fisher Unwin. Slave traffic, on my word of honor!—Thanks for your efforts with Mme. Pécher.[4] I haven't had

1. On 8 Oct., for on this date C. wrote to Unwin an unpublished letter (in the possession of Mr. B. J. Beyer) which refers to their conversation "of this morning." For this information we are indebted to Mr. J. D. Gordan.

2. Supposedly W. H. Chesson and Edward Garnett. But the latter describes his first meeting with C. as taking place at the National Liberal Club in November of this year (*Lrs. from C.,* pp. 2–5).

3. The word "proof-sheets" is in English.

4. Of Brussels. Her husband's cousin was a member of the Antwerp shipping firm of this name. See App. III, no. 2, and L. 11, n. 4.

time to busy myself much with maritime affairs, for Almayer came to pay me a three-day visit. He leaves today. Nothing to revise.

It would be very nice to come to Paris to see your pastel.[5] Nothing but the pastel, you understand. Not you; oh no, not at all! But I am much afraid that this pleasure is not for me. Not this year, at least.—When do you start appearing in the *Revue?*[6] I am beginning to hunger after your work. I embrace you heartily, and am ever your affectionate nephew,

J. CONRAD.

76. LONDON, 23 OCTOBER 1894.

23 Oct., '94. 17 Gillingham St.

Dear Aunt,

I have received your letter about leaving Brussels and have acted accordingly. M. Pécher now has all the necessary details. Thanks ever so much for your kindness.

I have nothing new to tell you. I have not been sent the proofs of "Almayer," but I am going to hurry those people up. I don't doubt that you will have the advance sheets[1] towards mid-November.[2]

The other work proceeds very slowly. I am very discouraged. The ideas don't come. I don't *see* either the characters or the incidents. To tell the truth, I am preoccupied with my plans for leaving, and as they don't seem to be working out I am in a constant state of irritation which does not allow me to lose myself in my story. Consequently my labors are worthless.

And you? What are you going to do? I have just reread *Le fils Grandsire* as a result of opening the book at random; continuing in this fashion, I read everything without skipping a word. I certainly love this book with an odd, wholly

5. By a Dutch artist, Schaken, and now at the Château de Montgoubelin, St. Benin d'Azy, Nièvre, the home of Jean Gachet. (Letter of Mlle. Alice Gachet.) For an earlier reference to this portrait, see L. 32.

6. Another inquiry about *Marylka* (cf. L. 72).

---

1. The two words are in English.

2. He did not receive the first sheets until late December (L. 81).

sentimental affection. I find you present on each page as I love you best.

Health pretty good. A hearty embrace. Your

J. CONRAD.

77. LONDON, 29 OCTOBER OR 5 NOVEMBER(?) 1894.

This letter appears to succeed L. 76. In L. 76 he had asked Mme. P. about her literary plans; he is now answering her reply. And because he is answering at once, we may perhaps take the liberty of supposing that the interval between L. 76 and this present letter was probably brief; that, in other words, she herself had answered L. 76 with fair promptness. If this supposition is correct, the Monday of the heading must have been either 29 Oct. or 5 Nov.

Monday morning.

Dear Aunt,

I am answering your dear letter at once. The idea for the novel[1] pleases me immensely. I am very happy to know you are busy creating with pleasure. That is a kind of guarantee of success.

I have already thought, several times, that you were doing yourself a disservice in offering to translate "Almayer." Since you have in hand a work which promises so well, you must no longer consider it. I speak very seriously and with conviction. It would be most unjust to you and to your creative art. They will doubtless send you the advance sheets,[2] but I beg you to lay them aside.[3] If I may be allowed to judge by myself, it would be unbearable for me to give up a work near my heart to—translate! Don't do it. It would be a crime.

You need for your novel a climax not only dramatic but characteristic. Have you one? A little Polish clerk is not like a little French clerk (how well Maupassant knew them!), and if you clearly grasp the difference (as I don't

1. *Pour Noémi.* See L. 94, n. 2.
2. The two words are in English.
3. On 12 Mar., 1895, C. wrote to Unwin from Brussels that Mme. P. was too unwell to undertake the translation (Keating, *C. Mem. Lib.*, p. 8). Over twenty years later a translation was made (*La Folie-Almayer*) by Geneviève Seligmann-Lui (*LF*, pp. 4 and 147).

doubt you do), you will achieve something fine. I suppose it will be rather the portrait of a woman, will it not?

You are too late with your advice, my dear Aunt. I am afraid I am too much under the influence of Maupassant. I have studied *Pierre et Jean*—thought, method, and everything—with the deepest discouragement. It seems to be nothing at all, but the mechanics are so complex that they make me tear out my hair. You want to weep with rage in reading it. That's a fact!

Yes, it is true—one works hardest when doing nothing. For three days now I have been sitting before a blank sheet of paper—and the sheet is still blank except for a "IV"[4] at the top. To tell the truth, I got off to a bad start. It comforts me somewhat to think that you have got off to a good one. But what can you expect; I don't feel the slightest enthusiasm. And that's fatal.

Serious criticism is treating *The Heavenly Twins* by Mrs. Sarah Grand[5] with the contempt it deserves. But, notwithstanding this, the book has gone through ten editions and the author has pocketed 50,000 francs. The world is a foul place. This woman is, besides, unbalanced, and stupid into the bargain. Try to imagine an imbecile gone mad. It is tragic and frightful. A real nightmare, indeed!

Mrs. M. Woods[6] has stolen my title. She has just published a book called *The Vagabonds,* and here I am in a pretty stew. Yes indeed! If you realized how this annoys me, you would pity me.

As for the idea for that book now without a title, since you have outlined yours to me I want to outline mine to you. First, the theme is the boundless, mad vanity of an ignorant man who has been successful but is without prin-

4. Because the chapter divisions of *An Outcast of the Islands* were considerably changed before the book was published, one cannot determine just what part of the completed work is referred to here. See L. 81, n. 2, and *LL,* I, 181, n. 1.

5. 1893 (Heinemann, London). For its popularity and its reception by the critics, see Whyte, *Heinemann,* pp. 104–106. "Mrs. Sarah Grand" was the pseudonym of Frances Elizabeth (Clarke) McFall.

6. Mrs. Margaret Louisa (Bradley) Woods. C. has incorrectly written "Wood."

ciples or any motive other than the satisfaction of his own vanity. Nor is he faithful even to himself. Whence the fall, the man's sudden descent into physical enslavement by an absolutely savage woman. I have seen that! The catastrophe will be brought about through the intrigues of a little Malay state, where the last word is poisoning. The dénouement is suicide,[7] still through vanity. All this will be merely sketched, as I am writing for the "Pseudonym Library" and will be limited to a volume of 36,000 words.[8] There you are.

Nothing yet from Antwerp. I am in negotiation with some Liverpool people. They have such a pretty little ship, and she has such a pretty name: "Primera"![9] I think this will go through, but I am sure of nothing.

Your letters are such a joy to me. After all, you are the only one in the whole world to whom I can tell everything, and your sympathy is so much the more precious to me on this account. Yours with all my heart,

J. CONRAD.

78. LONDON,
14 OR 21 NOVEMBER(?) 1894.

C. is now answering Mme. P.'s reply to L. 77, in which he had raised a question concerning the plot of her new work (*Pour Noémi*). Since Lrs. 78–80 clearly precede L. 81 (dated 27 Dec., 1894), and a "long silence" separates L. 78 from L. 79, probably the interval was not long between L. 77 and this one. Its date, then, would appear to be 14 or 21 Nov.

Wednesday, '94.

Dear Aunt,

I read your letter with astonishment and also with admiration. What fairy has given you the power of thus visualizing the complex events of life as they unfold in

7. No poisoning occurs in *An Outcast of the Islands,* and at the end Willems is shot by Aïssa (p. 360).

8. The book ran to over twice this length and was not published in this series.

9. An iron bark of 619 tons built in Glasgow in 1875 and owned by W. Sherwen & Son. See *Lloyd's Register of British and Foreign Shipping* for 1 July, 1894, to 30 June, 1895, under "Sailing Vessels," no. 650.

space and time? The history of your characters is thoroughly interesting. There is an abundance of situations. So you have only to let your pen run on.

I have had a long interview with Mr. T. Fisher Unwin. The work will surely not be set up in type before February of next year.[1] It makes no difference whatever to me. I have nothing to change in the way of style or structure; and as for misprints, the firm's proof-readers will take good care of them. I hope with all my heart and soul not to be in London at that time.

My work is not advancing, and my health is less good than it was. If I stay ashore much longer, everything will, alas, be spoiled. Tomorrow I am going to Antwerp on business, and I believe I may venture to call on M. Victor Pécher. It is too late to ask your advice, as the trip was decided on very suddenly only an hour ago.

Last Saturday I spent the evening with one of my friends.[2] We chatted a little about everything, including *Yaga*. He knows the book better than I. We recalled scenes which gripped us; we argued about them; and we also admired many passages with touching unanimity. We were critical, too. Very severely so; if you only knew how much, you would tremble! Afterwards I dug up my album and we considered the author's portrait while puffing clouds of tobacco-smoke with exemplary solemnity. The conclusion at which we arrived is that book and author are so-so —tolerable, very tolerable. Don't open your eyes so wide, Madame. I am joking. We said it was very beautiful,[3] and we said it with the most perfect sincerity. You are sure of at least two readers whose hearts you have touched—and not just upon the surface, but to their very depths.

A hearty embrace. Ever yours,

J. CONRAD.

1. But cf. L. 81.

2. Perhaps Edward Garnett. See his *Lrs. from C.*, pp. 5–10. But note that C.'s letter to him of 4 Jan., 1895 (p. 31) appears to have been written prior to Garnett's first visit to C.'s lodgings.

3. See Jessie Conrad, *C. and His Circle*, p. 70: "She [Mme. P.] was, I think, the most beautiful woman I had ever seen." Mlle. Aniela Zagórska has informed us that Charles Zagórski expressed a similar opinion.

MME. MARGUERITE PORADOWSKA

This photograph, by Klary, Brussels, appeared in the Revue encyclopédique *for 1896*

79. London, 26 November or 3 December(?) 1894.

The statement that he did not go to Antwerp as planned places this letter next in order to L. 78, for in L. 78 he told her that he was leaving for Antwerp the next day. The "long silence" would therefore point to late November or early December.

Monday. 17 Gillingham St.

My dear Aunt,

Forgive my long silence. I should have replied to your good letter long ago, but I had nothing new or interesting to say. And that is the case right now. This is only to tell you I still exist.

I have had no news from Antwerp. I must tell you I did not go as I had planned. There were obstacles. An affair which looked very promising fell through at the last moment. I choked over the disappointment for a whole week. .

It is sweet for me to think of you laboring unhampered and joyfully at the interesting work[1] the plan of which you described to me. As for myself, I am entirely bogged down. For a fortnight now I have not written a single word. It's all over, I'm afraid. I feel like burning what there is. It is all very bad; yes, too bad! This is my deep conviction and not a cry of stupid modesty. I have been floundering about like this for a long time. There you are! Nothing new. Nothing at all. Only much gloom. Health not bad.

A hearty embrace. Ever your devoted

J. Conrad.

80. London, 6 or 13 December(?) 1894.

The words, "I have burnt nothing. One talks like that . . .," place this letter after L. 79, in which he had written, "I feel like burning what there is." The fact, too, that he is immediately answering her reply to L. 79 suggests that the interval between L. 79 and the present letter was not long. Probably, then, the Thursday of the heading was 6 or 13 Dec.

Thursday. A quarter before midnight.

Dear Aunt,

I have just come in to find your letter. I take up my pen at once to reply while its impression is still fresh.

First, in general terms: very good! Next, as to the de-

1. *Pour Noémi.*

tails, I tell you honestly, sincerely, as friend to friend, that the idea for the first chapter is very good—very pleasing and effective. The development of the plot seems to me absolutely flawless. I foresee many dramatic situations. It is up to you to make them gripping, and I give you my word I believe in all conscience that you will be entirely equal to the task, for one does not construct such a framework without having a conception of the details. Detail is the most important thing in a novel such as the one you have in mind. And for a Polish story I see you are on the right track, for your women are to have much more character than the men, which is unquestionably true with us. I am sure that if you begin to write according to the plan you sent me, your characters will take their fate into their own hands. They will unquestionably be living people, for the events will inspire them. I congratulate you with all my heart—and I am a little envious.

I have burnt nothing. One talks like that and then courage fails. People talk this way of suicide! And then something is always lacking; sometimes it is strength, sometimes perseverance, sometimes courage. The courage to succeed or the courage to recognize one's impotence. What remains always indelible and cruel is the fear of finality.[1] One temporizes with fate, or tries to outwit desire, or attempts to juggle with his life. Men are always cowards. They are afraid of "nevermore." I believe that only women have true courage.

I am working a little. I agonize, pen in hand. Six lines in six days. What do you think of that? Fine, eh? I embrace you heartily.

J. Conrad.

81. London, 27 December 1894.

27 Dec., 1894. 17 Gillingham St.

My very dear and charming Aunt,

Ever so many happy wishes for the New Year, and success to the new book! So saying, I embrace you heartily.

I think of you so often! Every day. And I imagine I see

1. Cf. the similar thought in *AF*, p. 151, ll. 17–21.

you, pen in hand, the lamplight on your pensive head, the white sheet of paper before you, and your imagination working as it causes to live in joy or suffering all that world of bodiless souls beneath your forehead! You must be very happy. You see your work; I, I grope about like a venturesome blind man.

The decision is made. I have changed my title. It will be:

"An Outcast of the Islands."[1]

And the work itself is changed. Everything is changed except my doubt. Everything—except the fear of those shades which one himself calls forth and which so often refuse to obey the brain that created them.

Well, here is Chap. VIII finished. Four more to go![2] Four centuries of agony, four minutes of delight, and then the end—an empty head, discouragement, and eternal doubt.

Send me a note when you have time. Nothing but a word. Tell me of yourself and of your novel. Two words.

Ever yours,

J. CONRAD.

Received first proof of *Almayer's Folly* Christmas Eve (16 pages). I have had a horror of it. Absolute horror of the printed thing, which looks so stupid; worse—senseless.

82. LONDON, 30 JANUARY OR 6 FEBRUARY(?) 1895.

Pen, ink, and handwriting tend to place this letter not earlier than the fall of 1894. Hence the "XI" evidently refers to *An Outcast of the Islands*, Chap. VIII of which had been completed by 27 Dec., 1894 (L. 81). Allowing for the completion of two more chapters of the first, much shorter version (L. 77) now being written, as well as for the "long silence," we may tentatively assign the letter to late Jan. or early Feb., 1895.

Wednesday. 17 Gillingham St., London, S.W.

My dear Aunt,

I shall not ask pardon for my long silence. You know it is not because I have not thought of you, for you must

1. In English.

2. The novel eventually contained twenty-six chapters, with each of the five parts beginning with a Chap. I.

realize I think of you every day. But I have been sunk in the discouragement which everyone knows but which knows me better—I think I do not say this out of vanity—than anyone else.

Have you been working? Are you happy in your work? These are the questions that occur to me every day and that a note from you could settle, one fine morning. It is not that I wish to steal your so precious time, but I may well ask of you two or three lines, as charity. Charity, sweet lady! Surely there is no ban on this sort of begging!

As for me, *tout passe, tout lasse.*[1] I have just written "XI" at the head of a blank sheet, and blank it will remain for perhaps ten days, or I don't know myself. You see what my idea of work is. A funny one, isn't it? I have not been very well this fortnight. No sleep, no appetite; not really ill, though.

I embrace you heartily.

Yours,

J. Conrad.

83. London, 23(?) February 1895.

The first sentence of the third paragraph places this letter prior to 1 Mar. The reference to *Marylka* also places it later than the appearance of the first installment of this novelette in *RDM* for 15 Feb. The most probable date would therefore seem to be Saturday, 23 Feb.

Saturday. 17 Gillingham St., London, S.W.

Dear Aunt,

To explain why I have not yet thanked you for "Marylka" I must tell you I was in bed, in rather bad shape, at my friend Hope's[1] while your book[2] awaited me in London. I came back only yesterday.

My dear and good Aunt, you have butchered this poor

1. A favorite expression of C.'s. Cf., e.g., *Notes on Life and Letters,* p. 67.

---

1. At Stanford-le-Hope, Essex (Jessie Conrad, *C. and His Circle,* p. 42).

2. Since *Marylka* was not published in book form until 1896 (Hachette, Paris), C. must be referring to its presence in *RDM*. Evidently, too, he had received only the first of the three installments, which contains the scene here commented on. See *supra,* introd.

book! And Brunetière,[3] who is alone responsible, is, besides, an imbecile. But what remains is very charming, and there is spaciousness and the surge of wind in your description of the Ukrainian fields. It's astonishing! You have never been there, have you? I believe I am not mistaken in thinking that the scene between father and daughter[4] has been shortened. Isn't that so? It is all good, very good—without any flattery. Nevertheless I should like to shorten Brunetière by, say, a head. (The imbecile!)

Almayer comes out the first week of March.[5] "The Outcast, etc., etc." goes on its petty way amidst the usual weeping and gnashing of teeth. It is in my nature to be a miserable creature—a moral pauper, bankrupt of courage. I was to leave for Newfoundland on business,[6] but I don't feel well enough and the trip is postponed.

Write me when you feel inclined. I embrace you heartily.

Ever yours,

J. CONRAD.

You know my worship of Daudet.[7] Do you think it would be ridiculous on my part to send him my book—I who have read all his books under every sky? It is not that I expect him to read it, but simply to pay him homage, for after all he is one of my youthful enthusiasms that has survived, and even grown.

What do you think about this? Tell me how your book is progressing. I should like to continue my journey all the way to Passy—to see the manuscript.

My publisher is talking of a French edition. What ought I to do?

Oh heavens, how black, black, black everything is. This is one of my bad days. Pay no attention. Kisses.

3. The distinguished editor of *RDM*. See L. 29, n. 8, and *Larousse du XXe siècle*, I, 893.

4. Pt. IV (*RDM* for 15 Feb., 1895, pp. 862–866).

5. But cf. L. 85, n. 1.

6. Nothing further seems to be known of this project.

7. In 1898 C. wrote an appreciation of him that is in *Notes on Life and Letters*, pp. 20 ff.

84. London, 2 April 1895.

2 Apr., 1895.

My dear Aunt,

I don't understand at all. This is the first letter I have received from you since my departure.[1] I have just returned from Elstree,[2] where I spent ten days, four of them in bed. I am replying at once, for I am very disturbed. You are evidently sick at heart because you have overworked your body. Hence your disgust and discouragement. I feel for you, for I know that nothing is more painful than the inmost despair which torments you. One is so alone. What can I write? Nothing but words of genuine affection. Your letter has completely upset me.

I tell you that your novel is good, that the plan and the idea are excellent. In my letter which was lost I spoke to you of "Marylka." I told you how gripping the wedding-scene[3] is. I spoke too of the quiet, tranquil conclusion, with its promise of peace. It is very fine indeed. But the next book will be excellent. I feel it. I am sure of it. Courage. You have a very rich field there—situations into which you can put all your charm and all your strength. Your heart will speak of itself, I am sure; yes, certain!

I have got the book.[4] I shall send it tomorrow. Think of me who love you dearly, who suffer and rejoice with you. In haste.

Ever yours,

Conrad.

My respects to your mother. I was very sorry to hear of her illness. The fact is, I left feeling rather uneasy about her, and I wondered every day . . . however, everything is all right now.

1. From Brussels, where he had spent about a week in early March. See Garnett, *Lrs. from C.*, pp. 33 f.; also *supra*, L. 77, n. 3.

2. At the Sandersons'.

3. Pt. XXIII (*RDM* for 15 Mar., 1895, pp. 451–453).

4. An advance copy of *AF*. See L. 85. The copy presented by C. to his future wife, Miss Jessie George, which is in the Conrad Memorial Library at Yale, bears an inscription of which the date appears to be 21 Apr., 1895. Possibly, however, it is 2 Apr., 1895, the date of this present letter.

85. London, 12 April 1895.

Obviously 1895 because of the unmistakable references to *AF* and *An Outcast of the Islands.*

Good Friday. 17 Gillingham St., London, S.W.

Dear Aunt,

Thanks for your kind letter, in which you say so many charming things. I am very happy to learn that the book pleases your mother and sister-in-law.

I am not yet published, but shall be this month for certain. They cannot yet give me the exact date.[1] The Macmillan Company of New York is undertaking the publication in America, and because of the copyright-law we must wait until they are ready over there.

I have reached my seventeenth chapter. There will be twenty of them, I believe, if not twenty-one.[2] I am giving good measure this time.

I see you are better. I can perceive this from the tone of your letter, and it does me good. I don't need to urge you to have courage, more courage, and always courage. I am convinced you are at work on a fine book. A fine book! And you see it clearly from many angles. It remains now to choose a definitive point of view. Once the decision is made, please inform me of it without delay. I think as often of your novel as of mine. Oftener, perhaps. I don't exaggerate; that's the truth! I embrace you warmly.

Ever yours,

J. Conrad.

86. London, 30 April 1895.

30 Apr., 1895. 17 Gillingham St., S.W.

My dear, good Aunt,

I am not at all well. I am leaving my bed and setting out for Champel to take the waters and regain my health. This explains my long silence. You know that when I am not well I have attacks of melancholy which paralyze my mind and will. I have often thought, though, of you and your

1. Probably 29 Apr. See Wise, *Bibliog. of C.* (2d ed., 1921), p. 15.
2. Actually, twenty-six. See L. 81, n. 2.

book—*the book* to be. Once the general idea is settled on, you must let yourself be led by the inspiration of the moment. You are too much of an artist to go astray. *You* may be afraid of groping about in a blind alley, but *I*, who judge you "from without," am entirely unfearful of seeing you take a wrong turn. I have the utmost confidence in your inspiration, while I nevertheless realize that your doubts, your hesitation, are quite natural. How well I know them, my poor, dear Marguerite!

The idea of appearing in Polish is quite good. I doubt whether there will be any money in it, but you can try. So write to Angèle![1] I believe you are mistaken in your ideas on that score. Perhaps they did not receive the numbers of the *Revue*?[2] Who knows?

I have not yet seen Fisher Unwin about the translation. Today. Leave tomorrow. Will write you from Champel—next week.

Ever yours,

CONRAD.

87. CHAMPEL, 2 MAY 1895.

2 May, '95. Champel.

Dear Aunt,

I have just arrived here and feel better already. Drop me a line quickly to let me know how Calmann-Lévy[1] has answered your letter.

I have just written to F. Unwin to order the distribution of several copies of my book, and I have had one sent to M. Buls.[2] Write him a note saying the book comes from you. Otherwise he will be surprised.

1. Angèle Zagórska. See L. 2, n. 1, and App. IV. C. perhaps means that Mme. Zagórska might herself undertake the translation. See *LL*, I, 267.

2. Containing *Marylka.*

---

1. The Paris publishing firm. Probably *Marylka* had been submitted to it for publication in book form. (See L. 92, n. 3.)

2. Charles Buls (1837–1914), a burgomaster of Brussels and the author of several books on art and other subjects. See *Dict. des écrivains belges*, I, 167. He was a close friend of Mme. P., having, so Mlle. Aniela Zagórska has informed us, proposed to her both before her marriage and after her husband's death.

The Scottish papers (dailies) have begun to review my *Folly*. Short, journalistic, but highly laudatory! Above all, the *Scotsman*, a big Edinburgh paper, gets almost enthusiastic. The *Glasgow Herald* speaks with more restrained benevolence.

Now we are waiting for the London dailies, and *especially* the non-political weeklies. The first edition of 1,100 copies has been sold.[3]

That's all the news.

Tell me of yourself, of your work, of your plans.

I embrace you warmly.

Your CONRAD.

La Roseraie, Champel-les-Bains, Geneva.

88. CHAMPEL, 6 MAY 1895.

6 May, '95. "La Roseraie," Champel, Geneva.

Dear and kind Marguerite,

I have just received your letter. It gave me great pleasure. I can see you are better and, above all, tranquil.

That's it! Write, write. I want a dozen chapters ready for me to hear in Paris. I am stopping a day just for the novel—not for any other thing.

As for myself, I continue writing and there's no end to it.[1] I am afraid of prolixity, but I don't know how to avoid it.

Forgive my short letter; I love you none the less for it, you know.

Warmest embrace.

J. CONRAD.

You did wrong to tell Buls I sent it. Coming from you, it would be quite natural. From me, it is rather bold, don't you think?

3. But, according to Garnett, chiefly to the booksellers, many of the copies remaining on their shelves for years (*Lrs. from C.*, p. 16). See also Keating, *C. Mem. Lib.*, p. 6.

1. *An Outcast of the Islands* was evidently finished on 16 Sept., 1895. See Garnett, *Lrs. from C.*, pp. 39 f. Cf., however, *Lib. of John Quinn*, Pt. 1, p. 168.

89. Champel, 13 May 1895.

Obviously 1895.

13 May.

Dear little Aunt,

I send you the rough draft of the letter I am mailing by the same post to M. Buls.[1] When I see you in Paris I will show you his. It is most charming, gracious, and indulgent. I am literally quite bowled over by it.[2] And it is to you again that I owe this pleasure, a very great one. I kiss you —on both cheeks—and would do it for less. I am expecting a letter from you every day. And *the novel?* Speak. Write.

Ever yours,

J. Conrad.

90. Champel, 20 May 1895.

[*Printed letterhead:* Hôtels Beau-Séjour & Roseraie, Champel-les-Bains, près Genève; Champel, le]

20 May, [189]5.

Dear Aunt,

My warmest congratulations. I have seen nothing in the papers or I would, you may be sure, have written at once to tell you, or try to tell you, of all the happiness your success[1] has given me.

No *Figaro,*[2] but it is doubtless waiting for me in London.

1. This letter, which is in the collection, may be translated as follows:

Dear Sir, 12 May, 1895. Champel, Geneva.

It is very difficult for me to express the pleasure with which I read your so kindly letter. In sending you my book I surely had not the slightest pretension of occupying so much of the time that is precious to you and to others. I permitted myself at the most only to hope that you would glance at it in your infrequent idle moments.

I therefore felt a certain embarrassment on receiving your letter—that proof of the serious attention with which you have so kindly honored me. I assure you I am very conscious of my own small merit in this. Still, I persuade myself that, accustomed as you are to judge men and things—and with your good-will aiding—you have perhaps noticed that desire to do well which is the only motive in the world sufficient to excuse many errors, and all ambitions.

I hasten to write to my good Aunt to thank her also. It is owing to her that I have had the honor of receiving your criticism, and it is also through her that I am able to realize the high value of that criticism.

Yours gratefully and respectfully,

Jph. Conrad.

2. C. wrote to Unwin on 18 May (unpublished letter in Yale Lib.): "Mr. Buls (an artistic burgomaster) wrote me a warm letter of commendation." See also Garnett, *Lrs. from C.*, pp. 36 f.

---

1. *Les Filles du pope* (see L. 41, n. 1) had just won the Jules Favre prize of the French Academy. It was announced on 15 and 16 May. See *Le Temps*, Paris, of the latter date, and the *Revue encyclopédique*, VI, no. 169, p. 882.

2. See L. 91, n. 1.

If you will send your copy here, I will return it in a few days, when I am to have the pleasure of seeing you in Paris. I should soon be letting you know the date of my arrival.[3]

The whole provincial press has spoken kindly—and some papers enthusiastically—of my *Folly*. A big London paper has complimented me in a most pleasing manner. You will see all this—I have the clippings.[4] The critics, though, are yet to be heard from.[5] There are evidently some who hesitate to declare themselves, but the straws cast in the wind are moving in the right direction. I am working little, and badly, very badly.

And you? A moment of calm or a gust of contrary wind? —The change made in your chapter is very good. Wonderful idea. We shall discuss it at length, at great length. A good talk, I find, sends me back to work. Is it the same with you? If not, I shall be dumb as an oyster. I shall speak to you only by signs. You know! No Jonakowski[6] of any sort! Why did you fall, and why wasn't that imbecile Jonak there to catch you, since he is always hanging about when you don't need him?

I am pretty well. Not too well. Anyway, you will soon see.

Ever yours,

J. CONRAD.

91. CHAMPEL, 25 MAY 1895.

25 May, 1895.

My dear Aunt,

I have just received the *Figaro*. Ever so many thanks. I have read "Lemberg."[1] Why, it is charming! An absolutely charming narration in its liveliness and clarity of description. From the first paragraph to the last. Every-

3. See L. 91 and also L. 92, n. 1.

4. Sent by the publishers and also by an agency. See Keating, *C. Mem. Lib.*, p. 11.

5. A study of *AF's* reception by the critics has been made by Mr. J. D. Gordan. See *infra*, Bibliography.

6. For other references to this family, which cannot be identified, see App. III, no. 1, and L. 49.

---

1. A short travel-sketch ("Vers Lemberg") by Mme. P. in the *Figaro* ("Supplément littéraire") for 27 Apr., 1895.

thing is there. Everything! Well, did you, after all, go to that Exposition or not? I thought you had refused,[2] but I am beginning to have my doubts.[3]

I am coming to Paris about the 2d or 3d of June, but I shall write you before leaving Geneva. Forgive me if I close. I am not very well today. It is only temporary.

Ever your

J. C.

You make me curious about Gaba. What did she write? Must show me.

92. London, 11 June 1895.

11 June, '95. 17 Gillingham St., London, S.W.

My dear Aunt,

Pardon my infamous silence, but I have had so many annoyances! And also I didn't want to pass on to you the gloom of my troubles. I carried away[1] such a sweet and charming memory of you, happy and at peace in your nest among the birds.

I have set my affairs in order, at least for a while, and have gone back to writing, much encouraged by *seven columns and a half* in the *Weekly Sun,* in which T. P. O'Connor[2] buried me under an avalanche of compliments, admiration, analysis, and quotations, and all with an enthusiasm that caused him to make some quite absurd statements. That, however, sets one up, as the *Sun* specializes in this kind of literary notice—and I am pleased.

Tell me at once about Lemerre,[3] and about your work. Are you progressing?

I embrace you very heartily. Ever yours,

J. Conrad.

2. See L. 69.

3. For the most part, probably, because the above sketch (dated Oct., 1894) ends with an account of the Lemberg Exposition itself. But perhaps he is merely being facetious.

1. C. returned to London on 4 June (Garnett, *Lrs. from C.*, p. 37), having visited Mme. P. in Paris (see L. 91).

2. The well-known journalist and M.P. (b. 1848), who was now editor of both the *Sun* and *Weekly Sun.*

3. The Paris publishing firm. Probably *Marylka* had been submitted to it for publication in book form after being rejected by Calmann-Lévy (see L. 87, n. 1).

PART II

1900–1920

LETTERS OF CONRAD TO MME. PORADOWSKA 1900–1920

93.[1] Stanford, Kent, 16 April 1900.

[*Printed letterhead:*[2] Pent Farm, Stanford, Near Hythe.]

16 Apr., 1900.

Dearest and kindest friend,

This morning I received your letter enclosing Mother Odonie's, and this very moment I have finished a letter that I am sending to her at the convent in Lille.

After having thought some time about the word *entretien,* I made up my mind to write Mother Odonie frankly that if the word was the equivalent of "board" (in English) and only the tuition was to be free, my mother-in-law's means would not allow her to accept the Bernardine Sisters' generous offer. It is obvious that in a boarding-school like Slough that would mean at least thirty pounds a year for each of the little girls,[3] an impossible expense for a person who has literally nothing. As for myself, you know my means. It will be hard enough sledding to furnish them with even the most modest wardrobe. But if, on the other hand, *entretien* means the little current expenses, it might be arranged.

I thought it better to state the situation clearly, thus sparing good Mother Odonie the time and trouble of further correspondence. And it would, besides, be too bad for the children to go to Slough only to experience a disappointment they would feel keenly. Have I done the right thing?

1. A period of almost five years separates this letter from L. 92. On 24 Mar., 1896, C. married Miss Jessie George of London, whom he had met through his friends the Hopes (see L. 12, n. 3) in Nov., 1894. See *LL,* I, 163, and Jessie Conrad, *C. as I Knew Him,* pp. 25 and 101. This book and her later *C. and His Circle* contain numerous details of his courtship, marriage, and first years of married life. Many of C.'s letters of this period to Edward Garnett and others have been published.

2. On the left of the sheet is printed: "Station:—Sandling Junction, S.E.R."

3. The nieces of Mrs. C. The older child, Dolly, had been staying with the Conrads. See C.'s letters to Mrs. Stephen Crane of 25 Jan., 1898 (*The Bookman,* N.Y., May, 1929, p. 232) and 30 May, 1899 (*ibid.,* June, 1929, p. 371). The school at Slough was eventually decided upon (L. 94, n. 1; *LL,* I, 295).

My dear Marguerite, you have been most kind to the children and to us all. It is impossible to tell you how much we miss you! Borys[4] asked me this evening if you were coming back[5] tomorrow! He seems to expect your return every day. We haven't that consolation.

It is very late. I have sent Jessie to bed and stayed up to work. What a dog's life! It is wearing me out. I haven't even the strength to tell you how much I love you, how grateful I am for your firm friendship towards us—for your deep affection! Jess asked me to send you many kisses. The two little girls are filled with gratitude and affection towards you. I embrace you heartily.

Ever your

CONRAD.

94. STANFORD, KENT, 10 MAY 1900.

The heading of Mrs. C.'s letter (n. 1) provides the date.
[*Printed letterhead* (*as in L. 93*): Pent Farm, Stanford, Near Hythe.]

Dearest,

I am adding a few words,[1] chiefly to talk about the book. I have read the novel[2] religiously for the third time, from one end to the other. It is very good. Very good! The char-

4. C.'s oldest son, born 15 Jan., 1898 (*LL*, I, 223).
5. For Mme. P.'s recent visit to Pent Farm, see Jessie Conrad, *C. and His Circle*, pp. 70 f., and the postscript to L. 94.

---

1. To a letter in English from Mrs. C., which follows:

May 10th, 1900.

My dear Auntie,

Conrad's hand is better but he is dreadfully busy. I can never thank you enough for all you have done for the girls. I had a letter from Dollie last week and she said how very happy they both were in Slough. I enjoy your visit to us by simply looking back to it, and Borys often talks of his dear Auntie. When you write will you tell us what you can of Bruges. I am so looking forward to going there but even more to seeing you in Paris before the year is out. Mrs. Hueffer has another daughter nearly a month old. I am afraid they are both awfully disappointed it is not a son. Borys grows much quicker than I like and is quite a boy. Sometimes I heartily wish he were again a tiny baby; one feels more sure of children when they are very young, I think. When dear Conrad has finished his book we mean to take a little holiday. I will write again very soon

With love from all three of us

Believe me dear Marguerite

Yours very lovingly

JESSIE.

2. *Pour Noémi*, which appeared in *RDM* for 15 Aug., 1 and 15 Sept., and 1 Oct., 1899, and in book form (Plon-Nourrit, Paris) in 1900.

MRS. JOSEPH CONRAD IN 1896

acters are defined with a precision of which I am envious. The final scene is most touching to the very last line. I love the book. There is a very sweet charm in the style, and there is likewise strength. It all holds together; there are no loose ends. You know what I mean. Congratulations. As for its sale, we shall see. It seems quite assured to me, but the public is a fickle beast that grazes where it wills and prefers to feed on weeds. You will drop me a line to let me know how it is selling, won't you?

Hueffer[3] was especially struck by the delicacy of your artistic method. He is right in that. Besides, we minutely examined the dear book, which for us who refuse to discuss or even look at novels is an act of homage to your fine talent. He has just carried off *Yaga* and asks me to send his respects. I embrace you warmly.

Ever yours,

CONRAD.

P.S. The two little girls are in seventh heaven. Everyone is so good to them. These children surely owe you more than they can ever repay. I must say, too, that they are grateful to you, and Dolly especially is not far from adoring you. So is Jessie. You came like a good and charming fairy and have left your image in their hearts.

95. STANFORD, KENT, 16 MAY 1900.

"1900" has been penciled below the heading. It is undoubtedly correct, for, among other reasons, C. was in Bruges during the summer of this year (*LL,* I, 168).
[*Printed letterhead* (*as in L. 93*): Pent Farm, Stanford, Near Hythe.]

16 May.

Dearest,

How happy and proud I am! Yes, send the translation![1] I am dying to see it.

3. Ford Madox Ford, who had already begun to collaborate with C. See Garnett, *Lrs. from C.,* p. 168.

1. Of "An Outpost of Progress," which had appeared in *Tales of Unrest* (1898). See *LF,* p. 43.

I—better. Jessie—not very well. Borys—very well but naughty.

Thanks for the details.[2] We shall go to Bruges[3] or Neuport. We shall see.

Postman is waiting.

Ever yours,

CONRAD.

Kisses from everyone.

96. STANFORD, KENT, 1 JUNE 1900.

[*Printed letterhead* (*as in L. 93*): Pent Farm, Stanford, Near Hythe.]

1 June, 1900.

Dearest,

Yes, I received the manuscript.[1] Let me keep it for a few days, as I am just now very busy with my novel[2] and want my mind to be entirely free.

You are extremely kind.

In all haste.

Ever yours,

CONRAD.

97. LONDON, 15 DECEMBER 1904.

99 Addison Road, London, W. 15 Dec., 1904.

Dear and kind friend,

Last year I was ill all the time. Five attacks of gout in eleven months! Last December it was Jessie who, without being exactly ill, gave us serious alarm because of her heart. Scarcely able to walk myself, I took her to London (in January) to consult the doctors. They reassured me somewhat, but just as we were getting ready to return home to Pent Farm she had a terrible accident, a fall in the

2. About Bruges. See L. 94, n. 1.
3. In July (*LL*, I, 295 f.; *LF*, p. 40, n. 2).

---

1. See L. 95, n. 1.
2. *Lord Jim,* which was finished on 16 July, 1900 (*LL*, I, 295, n. 3).

street dislocating both her knees![1] After six weeks of agony in London, we spent a miserable summer in the country; she, hardly able to drag herself about, I, writing night and day, so to speak, to finish my wretched book.[2] For I must tell you that, to crown it all, my banker[3] failed in February of this year.

At last, in September, with the book now finished, we went up to London. I took Jessie at once to a private hospital (Nursing Home),[4] where three weeks ago she underwent an operation on her left knee (the other having healed). Bruce Clarke, one of our most distinguished surgeons, operated. So far as one can now judge, it was a complete success. No complications have arisen, and I have just moved her here to our apartment from the Nursing Home.[5]

I have had her here since yesterday. She sends you many kisses. She is still in bed but, I repeat, on the road to *complete* recovery. I can breathe freely for the first time in two years! And at once I write to you.

During all this while I have been in a pitiable state of mind. Unable to work for a whole year, fearful as to the future, struggling with financial difficulties, I did not want to, I could not, grieve you with my complaints. What would have been the use? At last I am coming out of this, shaken, jolted, but having regained a little hope. I dare at last lift my eyes. And it is towards you that I look.

In the midst of all this, I have recovered my health as if by miracle. I have had only one attack of gout this year, and it was very mild. I must now make up for lost time and lost money. We have both been ordered (Jessie and I) to spend the winter in the south. We are thinking of going to Capri for four months as soon as Jess can bear the journey. Perhaps in a fortnight—who knows? We shall pass through

1. See Jessie Conrad, *C. as I Knew Him,* pp. 50 f., and *C. and His Circle,* p. 89.
2. *Nostromo,* which was finished on 30 Aug., 1904 (*LL,* I, 332 f.).
3. Watson & Co. (*LL,* I, 326).
4. "Nursing Home" is in English, both here and below.
5. For the events narrated in this paragraph, see *C. and His Circle,* pp. 89–91.

Paris! Will you be there in January? Once assured of your forgiveness, I shall let you know the date of our departure.[6]

Ever yours, with all my heart,

CONRAD.

98. LONDON, 2 AUGUST 1906.

14 Addison Road,[1] London, W. 2 Aug., 1906.

Dear Marguerite,

Another boy, whose name is John Alexander Conrad, and for whom I ask a small place in your heart.

He is not very large, but he is well formed. It all went off very well. At six o'clock I got up to go for the doctor, and at nine-thirty I made the acquaintance of my second son. He looked at me with kindliness, and now (at four in the afternoon) I already feel considerable friendship for him. His mother is very well and embraces you warmly. She is very calm and very happy. There is no reason to fear complications. She feels perfectly well.

Borys was quite surprised, but he extended to his brother the kindest possible welcome. He has already made a fair division of his toys and has given him half his dog,[2] which is a real proof of affection, I assure you. So the most perfect harmony reigns in the family.

As for myself, after the week of nervous tension which preceded the big day, I feel limp as a rag.

Since naturally I began with you, I still have fourteen notes to write this afternoon.

So I close, embracing you with all my heart, and for the whole family.

Ever yours,

CONRAD.

6. They left London on 15 Jan. (*LF*, p. 68) and visited Mme. P. in Marseilles during May (*LL*, II, 19; *C. and His Circle*, p. 103).

---

1. The town-house of the Galsworthys, which had been loaned to the Conrads. See Jessie Conrad, *C. and His Circle*, pp. 117–120.

2. "Escamillo." See *LL*, II, 36, and, for further details about this pet, *PR*, pp. 103–105.

99. Stanford, Kent, 7 December 1906.

[*Printed letterhead:*[1] Pent Farm, Stanford near Hythe, Kent.]

7 Dec., 1906.

Dearest, beloved Marguerite,

Jessie wrote you some time ago. I wonder if you received the letter. It was about an accident in the Alps, the newspaper account of which alarmed us. For the name of Jean Gachet was clearly there as one of the three victims.[2] But the Reuter's News Agency despatch said "members of the *German* Alpine Club." So? . . . I don't know what to think, and I hope with all my heart that this great sorrow has been spared you.

Since Jack's birth I have worked night and day, so to speak, to finish the novel begun in March at Montpellier. It is done.[3] And here we are on the eve of leaving again for Montpellier to spend the three worst months of the year 1907.

Our intention is to leave Pent Farm the 16th of this month (Sunday) at eleven in the morning and arrive in Paris at 6:04 in the evening. As I hate to knock about the city with my caravan (including John Alexander), we shall put up for the night at the hotel in the station, which, after all, is quite comfortable. Dear and kind friend, grant us the pleasure of seeing you that same evening, and dine with us at seven-thirty. We shall try not to tire you out too much with our babbling.

On Monday I have invited H. D. Davray[4] (of the *Mercure*) and his wife to lunch, and I have the honor to ask you also with your brother, to whom please extend our cordial

1. On the left of the sheet is printed: "Station: Sandling Junction, S.E.R."

2. C.'s alarm about her nephew was needless. See L. 103.

3. In Feb., 1906, the Conrads went to Montpellier (*LL*, II, 3), where in March he began *The Secret Agent*. It appeared serially in America from 6 Oct., 1906, to 12 Jan., 1907 (Keating, *C. Mem. Lib.*, p. 165). But much further work was required to prepare it for publication in book form (1907). See *LL*, II, 38, 52 *et passim.*

4. Journalist and critic (b. 1873), who translated several of C.'s works into French. See *LF*, p. 38 *et passim.* The editors are indebted to him for information about Mme. P.

greetings. We shall leave that evening at 10:40, as before. Write us a note saying Yes. We all embrace you warmly.

Affectionately yours,

CONRAD.

100. MONTPELLIER, 5 JANUARY 1907.

5 Jan., '07. Riche Hotel, Montpellier.

Dear Marguerite,

The children are delighted! Little John kisses his cat with genuine affection. As for Borys, your nice present is wholly to his taste. We shall soon go to Palavas to sail the boat on rough water.

Warmest hugs from everyone.

Jessie is busily at work on her little cook-book, for which Alston Rivers & Co. are offering her *700 francs.*[1] It is worth the effort, and besides she knows her subject thoroughly—that is, cooking for a modest household. It likewise affords her amusement. Ever so many thanks for having sent the two stories to Davray.[2] How good you are to me!

Davray has allowed me to make some changes in his translation of "Karain."[3] Will you permit me to do the same with "An Outpost of Progress" and "The Lagoon"? Particularly the latter needs to be shortened, to be made a little more concise, don't you think?

I have had a mild case of the grippe. I have not written six lines since we arrived here. It is hard to get to work after a month of absolute idleness.

I have the laziness common to all Poles. I prefer to dream a novel rather than write it. For the dream of the work is always much more beautiful than the reality of the printed

1. For this firm and its frankly expressed rejection of this book in a letter to Ford Madox Ford which was accidentally sent to C., see the amusing account in Ford's *Return to Yesterday*, pp. 232–240. The book was not printed until 1922 (Keating, *C. Mem. Lib.*, p. 392).

2. "An Outpost of Progress" and "The Lagoon"—both, with "Karain" and two other stories, in *Tales of Unrest* (1898)—were being prepared for a volume to be published under Davray's direction by the *Mercure de France*. But the project fell through. See *LL*, II, 39.

3. Regarding these changes, see *LF*, 83, n. 3.

thing. And English is, too, still a foreign language to me, requiring an immense effort to handle.

I kiss both your hands. Our dearest love to you.[4]

Yours affectionately,

CONRAD.

101. LUTON, BEDS., 1 JANUARY 1908.

[*Printed letterhead:* Someries, Luton, Beds.]

1 Jan., 1908.

Dear Marguerite,

Ever so many happy wishes from us all.

Thanks for your good letter. Since our return[1] I have been ill twice; still the gout. I got up just today, not wishing to begin the New Year in bed.

Since the month of September we have been in this new house. It is larger than the Pent and has an old walled-garden. The countryside, also, looks altogether different here. We live as far from the sea as it is possible to do in England.

Borys is at school,[2] where he is doing well; yes, very well. From Saturday noon until Monday morning we have him at home with us. The school is about four miles from here. Jack has a slight touch of bronchitis just now. He is beginning to walk, but as yet hardly speaks. Jessie suffers a good deal with her knee. She is as courageous as ever. As for myself, I am tired and dejected. It is very hard for me to work, and my affairs in general are not going well. My last book[3] had some success—the usual thing. Even a certain fuss was made about it; but as for its sale, it's the same old story. I am one of those who don't sell. And here I am in my fifties! But still! We all embrace you heartily.

Yours most affectionately,

CONRAD.

4. The sentence is in English.

---

1. From Montpellier and Champel in Aug., 1907 (*LL*, II, 55).
2. In Luton (L. 103).
3. *The Secret Agent* (1907).

P.S. I have written to poor, dear Angela.[4] She is another person who needs all her courage. I have had a good letter from her, but it seems her eyes are in bad shape.

102. Luton, Beds., 15 January 1908.

Though the month of the heading is so badly scrawled as to be indecipherable, the letter itself identifies it as January.
[*Printed letterhead* (*as in L. 101*) : Someries, Luton, Beds.]

15 Jan., 1908.

Dearest Marguerite,

I am going to bother you considerably with my little errand, but I must have peace in the household.

Imagine, if you can, that Jessie bought a ticket in the "Pochette nationale" at Montpellier. It's a lottery, you know. There was a drawing on New Year's. But it was found that the wheel didn't work properly, so another drawing was decided on. It was to have taken place the 8th. It is impossible for me to get the issue of the *Petit Journal* for the 9th of this month. I had promised my wife I would, but I forgot. Could you in some way find out what number won first prize? Perhaps your maid, by just asking at a tobacconist's in the Rue de Passy (tickets were sold at tobacco-shops, and they will doubtless have a list there), will restore my domestic peace.

I had a frightful attack of gout for Christmas. Better now. I am very busy with a novel[1] and a novelette[2] (this latter is Russian—the first time I have handled the subject). For the rest, my affairs are going badly—but I am used to this. Have you seen a criticism of my last novel[3] in the new *Revue?*[4] Right beside it is a review of a novel by my friend

4. Angèle Zagórska.

---

1. *Chance* (see *LL*, II, 63 and 65). It was published in serial form in 1912 (Keating, *C. Mem. Lib.*, p. 224).

2. "Razumov," which grew into *Under Western Eyes* (1911). See *LL*, II, pp. 64 f.

3. *The Secret Agent.*

4. C. appears to be mistaken here, for while *RDM* for 15 Dec., 1907, contains a review of two of Galsworthy's novels, there is no mention of anything by C. See *LL*, II, 67 and n. 2.

Galsworthy, who was introduced to you at Pent Farm[5]—do you remember? How distant all that is! Did you get my note written New Year's? Jessie and Borys embrace you warmly. John Alexander is well.

Yours,

CONRAD.

103. LUTON, BEDS., 5 FEBRUARY 1908.

[*Printed letterhead (as in L. 101)*: Someries, Luton, Beds.]

5 Feb., 1908.

Dearest friend,

Thanks for your good, long letter. I bitterly regret my negligence in not writing you, but truly life is so hard for me in one way and another that I often lack courage to hold a pen.

The house in which we are now living is much bigger than the Pent, and the countryside is quite different. But we are much nearer London: thirty miles instead of sixty-six. The express trains take thirty-eight minutes between Luton and St. Pancras; others, from forty-five to fifty, or even an hour and ten minutes (though only two are that slow). And there are about thirty trains in each direction every twenty-four hours. So you see that the service to and from the city is good; and as there is a train at twenty minutes after midnight which arrives at Luton at one o'clock, it is possible, at a pinch, to go to the theatre (by the 5:22) and get home to bed the same night.

But poor Jessie is hardly in a fit state for jaunts of that sort. Moving about is a complicated business for the poor girl. And I too am getting old.

Alas, there can be no question of our going to France this year. The affairs of my literary agent[1] are embroiled; and, as I owe him a lot of money,[2] I am expecting some pretty serious financial difficulties. We shall have to live very quietly. Besides, Borys is at the Luton school and we can-

5. In 1900. See Lrs. 93 f.

---

1. J. B. Pinker.

2. See *LL*, II, 66.

not interrupt his studies to travel. And as for leaving him here, we couldn't do that either, for his health still requires close attention. Rheumatic fever leaves its mark. He comes home every Saturday noon to stay until nine o'clock Monday morning. And as the school is only three miles[3] from us, Jessie feels easy about him. I am happy to tell you that he takes his work very seriously. He is a very fine boy; very loyal, a little melancholy, and of rather uneven temper, but with a great store of love for his family. He adores John Alexander, who reciprocates in his own way.

Poor child, he was very ill in Switzerland[4] with whooping cough. For three months he was like a corpse, between frightful fits of coughing. The least little complication would have carried him off. Now he is a sturdy rascal, and beginning to walk, though he doesn't yet talk much. He is much more boisterous than his elder brother ever was. Everyone finds him very charming. I too think he is very nice. He has light chestnut hair (a little coppery), dark brown eyes, very black lashes, and big pink cheeks. We spoil him badly. That's fatal. Everyone does it, including his papa.

Tell me, dear Marguerite, who that relative of Angela's is who is living in London? Is it an Unrug—Angela was born an Unrug or Unruh,[5] wasn't she? And what is he doing in England?

I think that for Mme. Gachet and her daughter[6] to live in London is not a bad idea. I was very much interested in all you told me about Jean. I often think of this young man, who as a child was so attractive to me. What exactly is he doing in Canada? Does he really intend to stay there? I am sure you would be happy to have him in Europe, nearer you.

I dare make no plans for the future. It looks rather sombre at this moment. But you must come and see us, dear

3. Cf. the "about four miles" in L. 101. In both instances C. gives this distance in kilometers.

4. That is, John Alexander at Champel, following the sojourn in Montpellier. See *LL*, II, 50–52; Jessie Conrad, *C. and His Circle*, pp. 123–127.

5. The former is correct (App. IV).

6. Alice.

Marguerite. If I went to meet you in Boulogne, surely the crossing (seventy minutes) would not frighten you so very much. Keep it in mind for next summer when the weather is fine.

I close. We are about two miles from Luton, and the postman is drinking a cup of tea in the kitchen. The man is in a hurry. So, in haste, love and kisses from[7] Jessie (who is here), and from me too. Borys is playing today in a football match[8] against a Bedford school.

Ever affectionately yours,

J. Conrad.

104. Luton, Beds., 3 November 1908.

3 Nov., 1908. Someries, Luton.

Dear, good Aunt,

I have just received your card and will write by the evening post to Mlle. Alice Gachet, asking her to spend a day with us this week.

You speak of my success. Really it is not worth twopence. There have of course been some articles in the papers. In that respect, I count. That's clear. But truly I don't need their praise, and so long as the public will have none of me it makes no difference. For fifteen years now I have been writing, and at my age I may be allowed to be a little tired of it. But all this is not worth discussing.

Poor Jessie can hardly drag herself about. That knee is very bad. I am much afraid it will end with amputation one of these days. You can imagine that prospect adds little to the gayety (?) of our retired life.

Borys is quite well. He was badly shaken by two illnesses last year. But he is holding his own satisfactorily; he keeps up with his work and takes part in his schoolmates' games. John Alexander is in wonderful health. He is really very nice, with an impulsive character—Polish, you know—and a sharp little mind. Jessie will soon send you three little

7. The four words beginning with "love" are in English.
8. The two words are in English.

family photographs which are better than the group taken recently.[1]

I wonder what would happen to these poor creatures if I were no longer here. No family, no money, not even any acquaintances. I have ordered my life badly. I have not known how to do any better, for surely I have wanted to do the right thing. But perhaps it was impossible to do otherwise than I have done.

Jessie has just brought me the photographs for you. Here they are. She assures you of her deep affection and embraces you warmly. Borys often speaks of you. For all his faults, he is a fine little fellow. I have great confidence in him. Your ever loving and devoted

CONRAD.

105. LUTON, BEDS., 13 DECEMBER 1908.

13 Dec., 1908.

Dearest, beloved Marguerite,

I am deeply touched by your ever-watchful affection. It is exceedingly sweet to me to know that I am a little in your thoughts. Yes, truly!—of all the family I have only you left.

What does a Russo-Polish salon mean? Things, feelings, doubtless change, but I have not changed.[1] Oh, well! Still, it's strange.

Raychman[2]—that's a German name, and perhaps a little Jewish, eh? What will the lady write to me? What will she want to know?[3] If you knew how suspicious I am of interviews.[4]—Listen. You have seen her. You are able to judge if it is worth the trouble. After all, I have perhaps something to say. Decide for me, will you?

1. See *LF*, p. 93, and, for one of these pictures, Jessie Conrad, *C. and His Circle*, opp. p. 89.

---

1. One of many instances in C.'s writings of his lasting aversion to Russians. Cf., e.g., *LL*, II, 237.

2. Though C. has "Raychman," "Baychman" is probably correct. See the next note.

3. The collection contains a letter written in Paris by Davray on 27 Dec., 1908, to Mme. P. In it he promises to grant M. and Mme. Baychman an interview regarding C.

4. The word is in English.

I have just had a frightful attack of gout. Poor Jessie is suffering a great deal with her knee this winter. The children are well. Borys studies consistently and learns easily. The two meet seldom. The little one is still charming. We conceived a great friendship for Alice.

We all embrace you. Yours affectionately,

J. CONRAD.

106. ORLESTONE, KENT, 27 SEPTEMBER 1910.

[*Embossed letterhead:*[1] Capel House, Orlestone, Nr Ashford.]

27 Sept., 1910.

My dear Marguerite,

I have just finished a novelette and a short story;[2] I had to get to work at once after my illness, which, as you perhaps know, lasted four full months. Work has been so hard for me that, with the day's task done, I could not hold a pen or even think connectedly. You must pardon my long silence. It is not that I am lacking in affection. Please believe that you are always in my thoughts—always.

Without a doubt Jean has talent. You justly appreciate him. My letter to his mother was very short; I did not want to keep her waiting. I wrote my immediate impression upon finishing the manuscript. After all, dear Marguerite, it is up to you to pass on the question of whether this talent should be encouraged. You know him better than anyone else (I do not except his mother), you love him, you understand him; and he loves you and will listen to you. As for myself, I should never recommend a literary career to anyone. Besides, he is still young. He must wait and see. If he has the true calling, he will write in the face of all opposition. Then it will remain only to guide him in his literary

1. On the left of the sheet is embossed: "Telegrams:—} Station:—} Hamstreet."

2. The novelette was "A Smile of Fortune" (*LL,* II, 108 and 114 f.), which appeared in the *London Magazine* for Feb., 1911 (Keating, *C. Mem. Lib.,* p. 212). It was included in *'Twixt Land and Sea* (1912). The short story was "The Partner" (*LF,* p. 101, n. 1), which appeared in *Harper's Magazine* for Nov., 1911 (*Lib. of John Quinn,* Pt. 1, p. 184) and was reprinted in *Within the Tides* (1915).

development. And for that, with your solid judgment and the affection that binds you, there is only you!

Yes, dear friend, to move after eighteen years is hard! And the apartment at Passy[3] set you off so well! But still! We have had to move, too, the 22d of June. We like this house. It is surrounded by woods and is about four miles from Ashford and nine from Pent Farm, where you came to see us.[4] It is still the same Kentish countryside that we love so dearly.

Jessie suffers a good deal with her leg. Another operation is being talked of. She is resigned to it. The two boys are well. Borys is going to change schools next year. I should like to give him a term or two in France to learn the language. It is the only way. As for myself, I am getting better slowly—too slowly! But still I have gone back to work, and that is the most important thing. We all embrace you warmly.

Ever affectionately yours,

CONRAD.

107. ORLESTONE, KENT, 20 JUNE 1912.

[*Embossed letterhead* (*as in L. 106*): Capel House, Orlestone, Nr Ashford.]

20 June, 1912.

Dearest Marguerite,

Your good opinion of *The Secret Agent*[1] overjoys me. The book is not very characteristic of me, but I am fond of it because I think that in it I managed to treat what is after all a melodramatic subject by the method of irony. This was the artistic aim I set myself, for you well know that anarchy and anarchists are outside my experience; I know almost nothing of the philosophy, and nothing at all of the men. I created this out of whole cloth. It is very nice of you to have written Davray, who is a fine chap. He will be very happy.

3. See L. 24, n. 2. In 1920, as we know from the envelope of L. 110, Mme. P. was living at 10 Rue La Fontaine, Paris.

4. In 1900. See Lrs. 93 f.

1. Davray's French translation had just appeared. See *LF*, pp. 114–116.

The translation is really very good. As to the work's success, I have doubts. The public does not like irony unless it be served to them by a master hand.

Yes, dear and good friend, I have published a little volume of reminiscences[2] with a short preface. It has had a good press. It does not deal with the Ukraine more than with anything else. They are reminiscences connected with the inception of my first work and my first contact with the sea, which, as you know, took place at Marseilles, a city I shall always love with a very special feeling. I shall send you a copy at once. I beg your pardon for not having done this sooner, but I didn't know exactly where you were.

We are all in good health. Borys is a cadet aboard the training-ship "Worcester,"[3] though he has not the least intention of becoming a sailor. But it is a good school and he enjoys the life on board. He is doing well in his work. John Alexander is very nice, very lively—a genuine little heathen. Jessie will send you some photographs of the little monster, whom one can't help loving.

And when are you coming to see him, to see all of us who love you and think of you so often? Jessie greets you. Your very devoted and most affectionate

CONRAD.

108. ORLESTONE, KENT, 12 APRIL 1913.

[*Embossed letterhead* (*as in L. 106*): Capel House, Orlestone, Nr Ashford.]

12 Apr., 1913.

Dearest Marguerite,

It was a joy to receive your book.[1] Ever so many thanks. I have just finished reading it and have found it very

2. *PR*, which was first called *Some Reminiscences* (1912). It had appeared in the *English Review* for 1908 and 1909 (Keating, *C. Mem. Lib.*, p. 202).

3. Lying off Greenhithe (Jessie Conrad, *C. and His Circle*, p. 151). See also *LL*, II, 134 f. and 154.

---

1. *Hors du Foyer*, a novel which appeared in the *Correspondant* for 25 Feb., 10 and 25 Mar., and 10 Apr., 1912, and in book form (Éditions . . . du Temps présent, Paris) in 1913.

charming. I need not tell you how congenial to me your great talent is; and in those genuine and well-written pages I am very near you in thought and feeling.

Jessie and I have spent a very bad winter. Coughs, grippe, and all such horrors. I am a little better. Jessie is still coughing. Borys was in his school's infirmary for a whole month. And even John Alexander was ill for a fortnight.

I am sending this in care of your publisher, for I am not sure where you now are. We all embrace you lovingly. Ever your very devoted nephew and friend,

J. CONRAD.

P.S. John Galsworthy has spoken to me of you. He told me you looked well when he saw you at Davray's recently.[2]

109. ORLESTONE, KENT, 22 DECEMBER 1913.

[*Embossed letterhead* (*as in L. 106*): Capel House, Orlestone, Nr Ashford.]

22 Dec., 1913.

Dearest Marguerite,

This photograph[1] is not very good, but still it looks somewhat like me.

I wrote you in care of your publisher to thank you for sending your book.[2] Did they forward the letter?[3]

Our best wishes for the New Year.

We all lovingly embrace you.

Affectionately yours,

J. CONRAD.

2. Galsworthy was in Paris for four days beginning 18 Mar., and soon after his return to England he visited C. (Marrot, *Life and Letters of Galsworthy*, p. 365).

---

1. Probably the one that serves as a frontispiece to R. Curle, *Joseph Conrad* (1914). See *LL*, II, 148.
2. See L. 108 and its n. 1.
3. The envelope of L. 108 is preserved in the collection. The letter was forwarded to Mme. P. at 76 Rue de la République, Marseilles.

110. Bishopsbourne, Kent, 30 December 1920.

[*Embossed letterhead:*[1] Oswalds, Bishopsbourne, Kent.]

30 Dec., '20.

Dear Aunt and friend,

Our best wishes for this New Year.

We are leaving for Corsica about the 24th[2] of next month, there to spend two months. I am told the climate of Ajaccio is excellent. I want to rid Jessie of her bronchitis, which threatens to become chronic. After two years of suffering, with three operations (not counting three incisions), she is beginning to walk with crutches. Of course any movement is still rather hard for her, and that is why I have decided we shall not stop in Paris. We shall make the whole journey by auto, going via Le Havre,[3] Rouen, Orléans, and Lyons to Marseilles. Will you be there this winter? I dare not hope so, but it would be a great pleasure to give you a hug as we pass through.

John Alexander remains at school[4] and Borys at the wireless factory[5] where he started to work recently. We shall have only a nurse[6] with us.

I have just had a letter from Karola. She has been at Milan for three weeks.[7] I am sending you her address. I know that Madzia[8] has recovered and that Angèle[9] is in good health and working, it seems, in an office.[10] That is all I can tell you. Everyone here embraces you tenderly. I am ever, dearest Aunt Marguerite, affectionately yours,

J. Conrad.

Address: Mlle. Karola Ostoja Zagórska,
21 Via Libertà,
Care of Signore Sternieri,
Milan (Greco Milanese).

1. On the left of the sheet is embossed: "Telegrams:—Conrad, Bishopsbourne. Station:—Bishopsbourne, S.E.&C.R."
2. Actually, on the 23d (R. Curle, *C. to a Friend,* p. 96).
3. Actually, via Calais (*ibid.*).
4. At Tunbridge (*ibid.*).
5. At Mortlake (*ibid.*).
6. The English word.
7. Karola Zagórska left England for Italy in the summer of 1920. See *ibid.,* pp. 71 and 86.
8. Probably Mme. P.'s niece by marriage, Madeleine (Magdalena) Ołdakowska. See App. IV.
9. Aniela Zagórska. See App. IV.
10. In Warsaw. See *LL,* II, 262.

APPENDICES

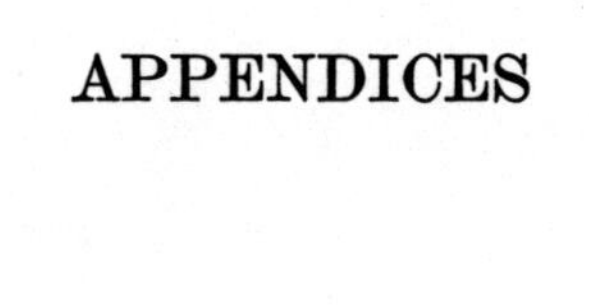

APPENDIX I

English Translation of Three Polish Letters from Conrad to Alexandre Poradowski

1

[*Printed letterhead:* The British and Foreign Transit Agency. Barr, Moering & Co., Shipping and Custom House Agents, 36, Camomile Street, London, E.C.]

16 Jan., [18]90.*

Dear Uncle,

I have just had a letter from Kazimierówka in which, replying to a question of mine, Uncle Tadeusz tells me you are residing in Brussels and gives me your address. I deeply regret not having known of this sooner, for I was in Brussels last October. It may happen, however, that I shall have occasion to visit that city again. The purpose of this scribbling is to recall myself to a relative whose kindness—shown to me in Cracow—I have by no means forgotten. I do not ask if you will allow me to visit you, for I permit myself not to doubt this, but I should like to know with certainty that you are in Brussels and that I can, in the course of the next month, find you there.

I returned to London six months ago after an absence of three years. Of these three years I spent one among the islands of the Malay Archipelago, after which, during the remaining two years, I commanded an Australian ship in the Pacific and Indian Oceans. Now I am, as it were, under agreement with the Société belge pour le commerce du Haut-Congo to command one of their river-steamers. I have not signed any contract, but M. A. Thys, the Company's manager, has promised me this position. Whether he will keep his promise and when he will send me to Africa I do not as yet know, but it will probably be in May.

I intend to visit Uncle Tadeusz soon; that is, I wish to do so and he himself also wishes it, but it is difficult, he says, in winter. I expect a letter from him in a couple of days which will decide the matter. If I do go home it will be via Hamburg, returning via Brussels. But should my visit be postponed, I shall at any rate go to Brussels in March in regard to the position in the Congo. So in

* In all three of these letters C. has written the "9" of "90" upon the second "8" of the "188" printed in the letterhead.

any event I shall have the pleasure of seeing you, dear Uncle, and of making the acquaintance of Aunt Poradowska, whom I know only from the portrait you had with you in Cracow.

In the meanwhile, dear Uncle, accept a very hearty embrace from your devoted relative and servant,

KONRAD KORZENIOWSKI.

A letter addressed in care of Messrs. Barr, Moering will always reach me.

2

[*Printed letterhead:* The British and Foreign Transit Agency. Barr, Moering & Co., Shipping and Custom House Agents, 36, Camomile Street, London, E.C.]

20 Jan., [18]90.

Dear Uncle,

Most hearty thanks to you and my Aunt for the kindliness shown in your letter. The sight of your handwriting delighted me inexpressibly, but, alas, my joy was of short duration! You greatly sadden me with the news of your poor health. Please do not trouble to answer this letter. I hasten to tell you that in view of your health I have decided to go home via Brussels. I know that after your operation you will need complete rest and not visits. Along with your letter, I received this morning a letter from Uncle Tadeusz, who says "Come." In the meanwhile those scoundrels in the Russian Consulate refuse to visa my passport; consequently there are new delays and vexations—visits to the Embassy, etc.—and perhaps nothing will come of it!?

I'll let you know how I'm getting along as soon as I've settled with these pirates. And so, au revoir, my best of Uncles. I kiss the hands of my kind Aunt. With all my heart, your loving nephew and servant,

KONRAD.

Please excuse the scrawl, but I have hardly time to catch the post.

3

[*Printed letterhead:* The British and Foreign Transit Agency. From Barr, Moering & Co., Shipping and Custom House Agents, Offices: 36, Camomile Street, London, E.C.]

31 Jan., [18]90.

My best of Uncles,

I already have the necessary papers and I intend to start from London next Tuesday—or, at the latest, Wednesday—and to go, naturally, via Brussels. I shall therefore be with you on Wednesday or Thursday, and, if you permit, I shall stop for twenty-four hours. Perhaps I shouldn't trouble my kind Aunt—particularly as you, too, are ill. I could sleep at a hotel, spending the day with you *s'il n'y a pas d'empêchement.* Upon parting we'll say au revoir to one another—and for only a little while, since I shall be returning via Brussels. Ever so many embraces. I'll come direct from the station.

Your affectionate

K. N. KORZENIOWSKI.

APPENDIX II

The Original French of Five of Conrad's Letters to Mme. Poradowska

The letters are here presented without critical emendation, for the mistakes they contain, though often mere slips of the pen, reveal much concerning C.'s manner of writing French. In striving to achieve absolute fidelity, however, we have at times found it impossible to distinguish between commas and periods, initial small letters and capitals (esp. *a, c, m, s,* and *v*), the verb endings *-ai* and *-ais,* and terminal *s* and *t.* When a reading has been doubtful we have tended to give the normal one. Underlined words have been set in italics; words and letters crossed out, and the lines under raised letters (in abbreviations), have been omitted; and occasionally a new paragraph is begun where C. has not marked such a division with indentation.

10

26 Sept^{re} 1890.
Kinchassa.

La plus chère et la meilleure des Tantes! J'ai reçu Vos 3 lettres ensemble a mon retour de Stanley Falls ou je suis allé comme supernuméraire a bord du navire „Roi des Belges" afin d'apprendre la rivière.—J'apprends avec joie Votre succès a l'academie dont—du reste—je n'ai jamais douté. Je ne peux pas trouver des mots assez expressifs pour Vous faire comprendre le plaisir Vos charmantes (et surtout bonnes) lettres m'ont causé. C'était comme un rayon de soleil perçant a travers le nuages gris d'une triste journée d'hiver; car mes journées ici sont tristes. Il n'y a pas a s'y tromper! Decidement je regrette d'etre venu ici. Je le regrette même amèrement. Avec l'egoisme d'un homme je vais parler de moi. Je ne peux pas m'en empêcher. Devant qui soulagerai je mon cœur si ce n'est devant Vous?! En Vous parlant j'ai la certitude d'être compris au demi-mot. Votre cœur devinera mes pensées plus vite que je ne saurai les exprimer.—

Tout m'est antipathique ici. Les hommes et les choses; mais surtout les hommes. Et moi je leur suis antipathique aussi. A commencer par le directeur en Afrique qui a pris la peine de dire a bien de monde que je lui déplaisai souverainement jusqu'au a finir par le plus vulgaire mécanicien ils ont tous le don de m'agacer les nerfs —de sorte que je ne suis pas aussi agréable pour eux peut-être que je pourrai l'être. Le directeur est un vulgaire marchand d'ivoire a instincts sordides qui s'imagine être un commerçant tandis qu'il n'est qu'une éspèce de boutiquier africain. Son nom est Delcommune. Il deteste les Anglais et je suis naturellement regardé comme tel ici. Je n'ai a esperer ni promotion ni augmentation d'appointements tant qu'il sera ici. Du reste il a dit que les promesses faites en Europe ne le tient guère ici tant qu'elles ne sont pas sur le contrat. Celles faîtes a moi par Mr Wauters ne le sont pas. Du reste je ne peux rien esperer vu que je n'ai pas de navire a commander. Le bateau neuf sera fini en Juin de l'année prochaine peut-être. En attendant ma position ici n'est pas nette et j'ai des ennuis a cause de cela. Enfin!—

Pour comble d'agrément ma santé est loin d'être bonne. *Gardez m'en le secret*—mais c'est un fait que j'ai eu la fievre en remontant la riviere 4 fois en 2 mois, et puis aux Falls (qui en est la patrie) j'ai attrapé une attaque de dyssenterie qui a duré 5 jours. Je me sens assez faible de corps et tant soit peu demoralisé, et puis ma foi je crois que j'ai la nostalgie de la mer, l'envie de revoir ces plaines d'eau salé qui m'a si souvent bercé, qui m'a souri tant de fois sous le scintillement des rayons de soleil par une belle journée, qui bien des fois aussi m'a lancé la menace de mort a la figure dans un tourbillon d'ecume blanche fouettée par le vent sous le ciel sombre de Decembre. Je regrette tout cela. Mais ce que je regrette le plus c'est de m'être lié pour 3 ans. Il est vrai qu'il n'est guère probable que je les finirais. Ou l'on me cherchera une querelle d'allemand pour me renvoyer (et ma foi je me prends quelquefois a le désirer) ou une nouvelle attaque de dissenterie me renverra en Europe, a moins qu'elle ne m'envoie dans l'autre monde, ce qui serait une solution finale de tous mes embarras! Et voilà quatre pages que je parle de moi même! Je ne Vous ai pas dit avec quelles délices j'ai lu Vos descriptions des hommes et des choses chez nous. En verité en lisant Vos chères lettres j'ai oublié l'Afrique, le Congo, les sauvages noirs et les esclaves blancs (dont je suis un) qui l'habitent. J'ai été heureux pendant une heure. Savez que ce n'est pas une petite chose (ni une chose facile) de rendre une créature humaine heureuse pendant *toute une* heure. Vous pouvez être fière d'y avoir réussi. Aussi mon cœur Va vers Vous dans un elan de gratitude et d'affection la plus sincère et la plus profonde. Quand nous reverrons nous? Helas la rencontre conduit a la separation—et plus on se rencontre plus les separations sont douleureuses. Fatalité.—

Cherchant un remède pratique a la désagréable situation que je me suis fait j'ai trouvé un petit plan—assez en l'air—ou Vous pourriez peut-être m'aider. Il parait que cette Compagnie ou une autre affiliée a celle-ci aura—(est même en a déjà un) des navires de mer. Probablement ce grand (ou gros?) banquier qui fait la pluie et le beau temps chez nous aura un large interêt dans l'autre Comp^{ie}.—Si on pouvait soumettre mon nom pour commander un de leur navires (dont le port d'attache sera Anvers) je pourrai chaque voy^{ge} m'echapper pour un jour ou deux a Bruxelles quand vous êtes là. Ce serait ideal! Si on voulait me rappeler pour prendre un commandement je payerais mes frais de retour moi même naturellement. C'est une idée a peine praticable peut-être mais si Vous revenez a Bruxelles en hiver, Vous pourriez par Mr Wauters savoir ce qui en est, n'est-ce pas chère petite Tante?—

Je vais envoyer ceci aux soins de la Princesse (que j'aime parce que elle Vous aime).—Bientôt probablement Vous verrez pauvre chère Tante Gaba, ces chers et bons Charles Zag^{ski} et leur charmantes petites. Je Vous envie! Dites leur que je les aime bien tous et que j'en demande un petit brin de retour. Mlle Marysieńka a oublié probablement la promesse qu'elle m'a faite de sa fotographie. Je suis toujours son cousin et serviteur très devoué. Je n'ose pas dire admirateur de peur de ma Tante Oldaknoska [?] a qui je me rapelle avec affection. Je Vous charge par tous les dieux de me garder le secret de ma santé devant *tout le monde,* autrement mon oncle sera sur de le savoir.—Je finis. Je pars dans une heure pour Bamou dans un canot, choisir et faire couper le bois de construction pour la station ici. Je resterai campé dans la foret 2 ou 3 semaines a moins de maladie. J'aime cela assez. Je pourrai sans doute avoir un ou deux coup de fusil sur les buffles ou elephants. Je Vous embrasse de tout mon cœur. J'ecris par la malle prochaine une longue lettre

Votre affectionné neveu

J. C. K.

32

16 octobre [1891].
Londres.
17 Gillingham St.
S.W.

Chère Tante.

Je me demande si Vous êtes très fachée contre Votre très paresseux neveu? J'aime a croire cependant que Vous avez le sentiment du devoir de l'indulgence, vu que l'existence n'est possible qu'en vertu de ce même sentiment.

Je n'ai absolument rien a Vous dire. Je vegète. Je ne pense même pas;—donc je n'existe pas (selon Descartes). Mais un autre individu (un savant) a dit: „Sans phosphore point de pensée". D'ou il semble que c'est le phosphore qui est absent et moi je suis toujours là. Mais dans ce cas j'existerais sans penser, ce qui (selon Descartes) est impossible.—Grand Dieux! Serai-je un Polichinelle? Le Polichinelle de mon enfance, Vous savez—l'echine cassée en deux le nez par terre entre les pieds; les jambes et les bras raidement écartés, dans cette attitude de profond desespoir, si pathetiquement drôle, des jouets jétés dans un coin. Lui n'avait pas de phosphore; je sais, car j'ai léché toute la peinture de ces joues vermeilles, embrassé, et même mordu, son nez bien des fois sans m'en trouver plus mal. C'etait un ami fidèle. Il recevait mes confidences d'un air sympathique en me regardant d'un œil affectueux. Je dis d'un œil car dans les premiers jours de notre amitié je lui avais crevé l'autre dans un acces de folle tendresse. Du reste il n'a jamais semblé s'en aperçevoir de peur de me causer de la peine. C'etait un „gentleman". Les autres polichinelles que j'ai connu depuis criaient quand on leur marchait sur le pied. A-t-on l'idée d'une impertinence pareille!? Après tout rien ne remplace les amitiés de notre enfance.—

Ce soir il me semble que je suis dans un coin, l'echine cassée, le nez dans la poussière. Voulez Vous avoir la bonté de ramasser le pauvre diable, le mettre tendrement dans Votre tablier, le presenter a Vos poupées, lui faire faire la dinette avec les autres. Je me vois d'ici a ce festin le nez barbouillé des confitures, les autres me regardant avec cet air d'etonnement frigide qui est naturel aux poupées bien fabriquées. J'ai été regardé comme cela bien des fois par des mannequins innombrables. Ma foi! Je leur pardonne; il y a eu un temps ou j'étais chrétien!—J'avais l'intention en commencant cette lettre de Vous dire que Votre costume de pose (pour le portrait) me plait quoique il m'est difficile de Vous imaginer dedans. Savez Vous que par une de ces charmantes plaisanteries dont le Destin et* si prodigue je ne Vous ai vue qu'en noir? Enfin! Qui vivra verra. Peut-etre je vivrai assez longtemps pour Voir Votre portrait.—

Je Vous embrasse de tout mon cœur. Votre très devoué

J. Conrad.

37

4 Sept. 1892.
Londres.

Très chère Tante.

Arrivé avant-hier j'ai eu le bonheur de lire Vos charmantes et bonnes lettres ce matin. J'ai trouvé toutes les lettres a Londres car

* One of C.'s most common slips of the pen.

mon ami Krieger etant très gravement malade personne au bureau n'a eu le bon sens de me les envoyer en Australie ou au Cap ou on savait bien que nous allions faire relâche. Je suis heureux de Votre bonheur (comparatif) ou du moins de la paix que Vous avez trouvée dans cette solitude qui Vous faisait tant peur. Malheureusement j'ai a Vous annoncer qu'il me sera impossible de rompre cette solitude car je serais très occupé et un congé et* tout-a-fait hors de question. Quand a quitter le navire je ne peux pas me permettre ce luxe a cause du pain quotidien—vous savez—celui qu'on mange a la sueur de son front—et quelquefois a celle d'autrui quand on a l'intelligence de rester a l'ombre et laisser les autres s'evertuer au soleil. Moi je ne possède ni cette intelligence ni cette chance—par conséquent Vous ne me verrez pas cette année ci a Passy.—Je Vous dis cela tout de suite car je Vous crois capable de deranger tous Vos plans pour Votre Vaut-rien (pas vaurien) de neveu.—Ce que Vous me dites de Jean m'attriste. Vous pensez déjà aux conquêtes qu'il fera et cœurs qu'il brisera. Comme c'est caracteristique individuellement et nationalement! Moi je pense qu'élevé de cette façon il grandira et mûrira sans realiser la significance de la vie avec une fausse idée de sa place dans le monde. Il se croira important. On se croit toujours important a 20 ans. Le fait est cependant que l'on ne devient utile que quand on realisé toute l'etendue de l'insignificance de l'individu dans l'arrangement de l'univers. Quand on a bien compris que par soi même on n'est rien et que l'homme ne vaut ni plus ni moins que le travail qu'il accomplit avec hònnêtété de but et des moyens et dans les strictes limites de son devoir envers la société ce n'est qu'alors que l'on est maitre de sa conscience et on a le droit de se dire un homme. Autrement serait il plus charmant que le prince Charmant, plus riche que Midas plus savant que le docteur Faust lui même l'être a deux pattes sans plumes n'est qu'une loque meprisable pietinée dans la boue de toutes les passions. Je pourrais gâter bien du papier sur ce thème là mais Vous me comprenez sans doute aussi bien que je me comprends moi même sans plus d'explications.—

Mon oncle a été plus ou moins malade tout l'hiver En été il se sentit mieux mais j'ai bien peur que cela ne durera pas. Du reste je me trompe peut-etre car je vois tout en noir depuis que ma santé n'est plus bonne. C'est bête mais c'est comme cela. Nous avons arrangé ma visite en Russie pour l'année prochaine et alors je passerai par Paris. J'espère donc Vous voir en même temps. Mais faire des plans est une occupation bien ingrate. C'est toujours l'imprévu qui arrive.—

* Note the same slip in L. 32.

Presentez mes compliments a Mme Votre Mère et a Mme & M Bouillot Je presume que Mme Votre Belle soeur et les enfants sont en Angleterre en ce moment.—

Je Vous remercie mille et mille fois du bon souvenir que Vous me gardez. Je ne sais vraiment comment j'ai merité Vos bonnes grâces, mais je les accepte comme on accepte les dons du Ciel; avec une humble gratitude, avec la conscience de mon indignité, sans tâcher de comprendre la Sagesse Eternelle.

Votre très devoué

J CONRAD

59

24 Avril 1894
11^{h} matin.

Ma chère Tante.

J'ai la douleur de Vous faire part de la mort de M. Kaspar Almayer qui a eu lieu ce matin a 3^{h}

C'est fini! Un grattement de de Plume ecrivant le mot de la fin et soudain toute cette compagnie des gens qui ont parlé dans mon oreille, gesticulé devant mes yeux, vécu avec moi pendant tant d'années devient une bande des fantômes qui s'eloignent, s'effacent se brouillant; indistincts et palis par le soleil de cette brillante et sombre journée.—

Depuis que je me suis reveillé ce matin il me semble que j'ai enseveli une part de moi-même dans les pages qui sont là devant mes yeux. Et cependant je suis content—un peu.—

Je Vous enverrai les Deux Chap^{tres} aussitot typés.—

Merci de Votre lettre

Je Vous embrasse de tout mon coeur.

Toujours Votre fidèle et devoué

J. CONRAD.

77

Lundi matin.
[29 Oct. or 5 Nov. (?), 1894.]

Chère Tante.

Je reponds tout de suite a Votre chère lettre. L'idée du roman me plait infiniment. Je suis très heureux de savoir que Vous êtes en train de créer avec plaisir. C'est en quelque sorte une garantie de succés.

J'ai déjà pensé—plusieurs fois que Vous Vous faites une injustice en offrant de traduire Almayer. Du moment que Vous avez un ouvrage qui promet si bien il ne faut pas Vous en occuper. Je parle très serieusement et avec conviction. Ce serait très injuste a Vous et a Votre art créateur. On Vous enverra sans doute les "advance sheets" mais je Vous en supplie mettez les de coté. Si je puis me permettre de juger par moi même—il me serait insupportable de quitter un ouvrage qui me tiendrait au coeur pour—traduire! Ne faites pas ça. Ce serait un crime.—

Il Vous faut pour Votre roman une catastrophe non seulement dramatique mais encore characteristique. L'avez Vous? Un petit employé polonais ne ressemble pas un petit employé français (come Maupassant les connaissait bien!) et si Vous voyez la difference clairement (comme je n'en doute pas) vous ferez quelque chose de beau. Je suppose que ce sera plutôt une etude de femme. N'est-ce pas?

Vous êtes trop tard avec Votre avis Madame ma Tante. J'ai peur que je ne sois trop sous l'influence de Maupassant. J'ai étudié „Pierre et Jean"—pensée, methode et tout—avec le plus profond déséspoir. Ça n'a l'air de rien mais c'est d'un compliqué comme mécanisme qui me fait m'arracher les cheveux. On a envie de pleurer de rage en lisant cela.—Enfin!—

Oui c'est vrai. On travaille le plus quand on ne fait rien. Voilà trois jours que je m'assois devant une page blanche—et la page est toujours blanche excépté pour un IV en tête. A vrai dire je suis mal parti. Je me console un peu en pensant que Vous êtes partie du bon pied. Que Voulez Vous? Je ne ressens le moindre enthousiasme. C'est fatal, cela.—

La critique serieuse traite les „Heavenly Twins" de Mme Sarah Grand avec le mepris qui lui est du. Mais!—le livre a passé par 10 éditions et l'auteur a empoché 50,000 francs. Le monde est un sale endroit.—Du reste cette femme est détraquée et bête par dessus le marché. Imaginez Vous un imbecile qui deviendrait fou. C'est d'un triste et d'un affreux. Un vrai cauchemar, quoi!—

Mme M. Wood m'a volé mon titre. Elle vient de publier un livre: „The Vagabonds" et me voilà joliment embêté. Non! Si Vous saviez comme ça m'ennuie Vous auriez pitié de moi.—

Quand a l'idée de cet ouvrage a présant sans titre comme Vous m'avez indiqué la votre je veux vous indiquier la mienne. Le motif d'abord c'est une vanité effrenée, feroce d'un homme ignorant qui a du succés mais n'a ni principes ni d'autre ligne de conduite que la satisfaction de sa vanité.—Aussi il n'est même pas fidèle a soi même. D'ou chute, degringolade subite jusqu'a l'esclavage physique de l'homme par une femme absolument sauvage J'ai vu ça! La catastrophe sera amenée par les intrigues d'un petit etat malais, dont le dernier mot est : empoisonnement. Le denoument est : suicide par vanité encore. Tout cela ne sera qu'esquissé car comme j'écris pour la „Pseudonym Library" je suis limité a 36000 mots pour faire un volume. Voilà.—

Rien encore d'Anvers. Je suis en negociations avec des gens de Liverpool. Ils ont un si joli petit navire—et il a un si joli nom! „Primera".—Je pense que cela aboutira mais je ne suis sur de rien.—

Vos lettres sont une grande joie pour moi. Au bout du compte il n y a que Vous au monde a qui je peux tout dire—et Votre sympathie est d'autant plus precieuse. A Vous de tout coeur

J. CONRAD.—

APPENDIX III

Two Fragmentary, Unsent Letters of Mme. Poradowska to Conrad

The spelling and punctuation have been somewhat emended, and underlined words have been placed in italics.

1

The second part bears the date of 9 June, 1890; and the first part, because of the reference to her husband's death, can be dated 7 June (see L. 2, n. 2).

—Il est bien tenace, et je me sens si peu outillée pour tout cela.—

Il y a aujourd'hui quatre mois jour pour jour, que j'ai perdu mon pauvre Olis, et lui justement qui aurait eu tant de joie de ce prix, plus de joie qu'aucune personne vivante, car Dieu sait comme il m'aimait, et comme chaque petite satisfaction morale que j'éprouvais, il la partageait et en jouissait bien plus que moi. . . . Lui n'est pas là pour me dire qu'il est content—alors . . . je me dis . . . à quoi bon. Mon Dieu, Conrad, comme c'est dur la vie, et comme on a beau faire—ce vide est toujours là qui nous guette. Voilà trois jours que je me bats les flancs pour être passablement gaie—et je ne peux pas y réussir; la bonne Princesse le voit sans doute car elle est encore meilleure, encore plus tendre. Je suis ingrate—mais c'est plus fort que moi . . . Ça passera, j'imagine, comme tout passe—et puis . . . ça reviendra . . .

Je vais écrire une très longue lettre à ma chère Gabrielle—

Pauvre petit Jean, maman m'écrit qu'il a tant pleuré quand il a su qu'Auntie était partie, car la veille il m'avait promis de venir à la gare—6 hres—il se leverait à 4 hres, il trouverait tout seul le chemin de chez Madame Bouillot! Et toute la journée il pleurait et disait—I want mon pétit tant'! . . . Pauvre bijou, à présent il est consolé. J'ai écrit à Bruxelles tous vos messages affectueux.

Toujours pas de fièvre? . . . Ah, je voudrais en être sûre mais ce livre du Congo est si peu rassurant!

9 juin 9°. Pauvre Conrad, j'espère que vous n'allez pas vous mettre dans la tête qu'il faut me répondre à toutes mes lettres et longuement—je sais que vous êtes un marin—et qu'il fait chaud —et que c'est ennuyeux d'écrire, moi . . . C'est 1° mon métier, et

puis, outre que je veux vous faire plaisir, j'éprouve une grande satisfaction à ajouter quand il m'en vient envie un mot à ce petit cahier. Ne répondez que quand votre bon cœur parlera et que vous aussi aurez envie de causer avec votre tante.

Quelquefois, en considérant ma vie qui désormais est ma propriété, j'ai l'impression d'avoir reçu tout à coup un immense cadeau, néfaste, encombrant, et dont je ne sais encore que faire, et j'ai envie de crier : reprenez-là !—

J'ai vue hier Josephine Syroczynska, Mme Rejska. Elle est assez bien sauf des dents un peu noires, mais toujours sa joile taille. Elle m'a reçue avec beaucoup d'amitié et de curiosité comme toujours, a parlé de sa mère qui élève les enfants de Marie,—de Técla qui est toujours malade; elle a même ajouté avec ce sangfroid imperturbable qu'elles ont toujours eu dans les circonstances les plus graves. Elle est poitrinaire (et sa mine semblait dire, elle n'en a pas pour longtemps).

J'ai vue sa fillette aînée, jolie mais tête carrée, et je me suis dit après ma visite un peu vide, un peu gauche, un peu froide, que vous aviez raison ! . . . Elle m'a parlé de vous, m'a dit qu'elle est votre cousine, que vous avez toujours aimé à lire les voyages de Jules Verne, etc., etc. C'est singulier de se dire qu'elle est votre cousine, elle vous ressemble si peu. Depuis cette visite, il y a des côtés de votre caractère que je comprends peut-être mieux. Je crois qu'une nature comme la vôtre devait s'exaspérer devant la froideur vertueuse et irritante de cette famille qui se croyait impeccable et qui n'avait aucune des qualités fermes qu'il faut pour élever un enfant ardent, mais qui a au fond de son cœur un grand besoin de tendresse et un profond sentiment de la justice; et j'ai si bien compris ça que c'est à peine si j'ai dit à Josephine que je vous avais vu, tant je devinais . . . qu'elle ne comprendrait pas. . . . Oui décidement, elle et moi nous parlons une autre langue.—

Les Yonakowski également m'ont fait demander d'aller les voir et les Léon arrivent avec le fiancé d'Hélène pour la cérémonie funèbre à l'occasion des cendres du Prés. Kiewicz qu'on apporte de Constantinople et qui seront déposées dans le tombeau des rois—

2

20, rue Godecharles
4 février 91.

Mon cher Conrad,

Votre lettre m'a rassurée sur votre santé, et je vous vois bientôt revenu complètement à votre état normal. Ces six semaines de pénitence sont bien longues mais vous ne les passerez pas toutes au lit, je suppose. Il ne faut pas voir tout en triste—bientôt la vie vous sourira de nouveau, vous reprendrez le commandement d'un beau navire, et encore une fois vous vous laisserez emporter par le courant. . . . Et je comprends si bien que d'ici au moment où vous ne serez pas sûr de tenir votre commandement, vous aurez le spleen, et moi qui vous prêche en ce moment, ne serai-je pas toujours en fièvre, énervée et agacée, tant que je n'aurai pas trouvé ce travail d'une part, et ce coin solitaire pour écrire, de l'autre.—Nos deux existences si différentes ont d'étranges points de ressemblance. Seulement vous êtes jeune, vous êtes un homme fort; l'avenir vous sourit. Moi je m'abêtis, je me sens de trop; les chagrins du passé me hantent. Je ne vois rien de tentant à l'horizon. Seul un travail bien dans mes cordes pourrait me fouetter le sang, au point de me faire encore jouir du présent.

Les deux journées que je vous ai vu ont été bonnes; depuis, je broie du noir; chaque jour de cette semaine me rappelle des larmes; et puis je me suis refroidie; je garde la chambre; je souffre; enfin je suis misérable.

Tout cela pour vous dire simplement que je n'ai pas eu le loisir d'aller chez Mme *Pécher* (s'il vous plait et non Pêchet). Aussitôt que je pourrai sortir je ne ferai qu'un bond jusque là, et j'emploierai toute mon éloquence à convaincre cette dame dont le mari est le cousin du Pécher d'Anvers, comprenez-vous?

Je lui énumérerai toutes les qualités dont vous faites mention et toutes celles que je connais moi—et qui ont échappé à votre modestie. Cette dame adore *l'Evêque;* vous savez, celui de Wolà, le mien—enfin le fameux. Vous pensez bien que j'aurai soin de lui lancer adroitement que l'évêque s'intéresse à votre sort. Et le fait est qu'il m'a demandé plusieurs fois avec beaucoup d'intérêt des nouvelles de ce neveu de mon mari qui était allé au Congo, et qu'il aurait tant voulu voir avant son départ.

APPENDIX IV

The Poradowski Genealogy

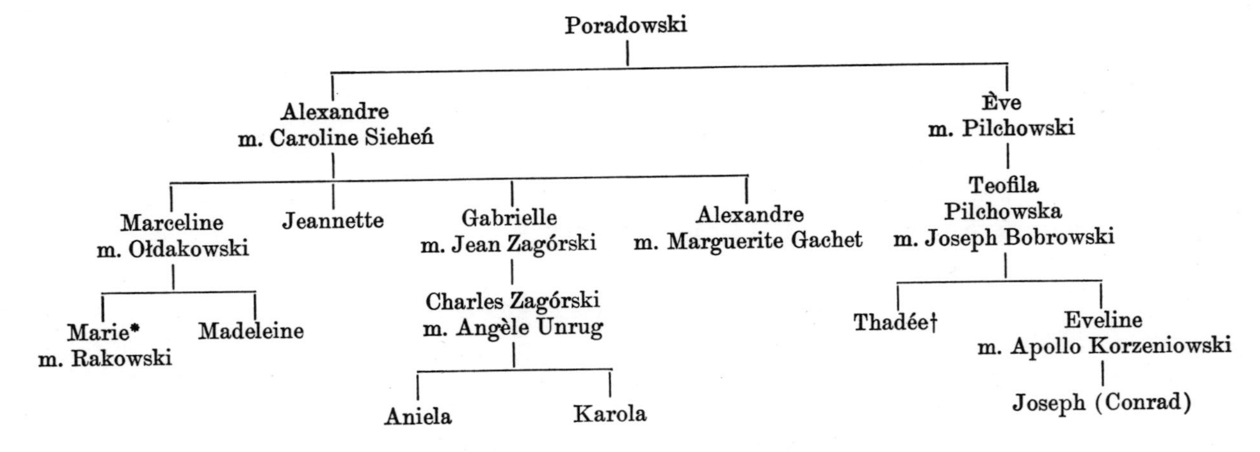

* Marysieńka (Lrs. 10 and 43). † There were six sons and two daughters (*LL*, I, 1).

APPENDIX V

The Paper of the Letters

Printed and embossed letterheads and noteheads are generally abbreviated in this list; they may be found in greater completeness by consulting the pages containing the translation of the letters. The size of the sheets is given in inches, with the horizontal dimension always coming first.

1. *App. I, nos. 1, 2.* Single letterhead (Barr, Moering & Co., etc.). 8.8 x 10.8. Bluish grey. Wove paper, reinforced by gauze.
2. *App. I, no. 3.* Half letterhead (Barr, Moering & Co., etc.). 9.7 x 7.7. Blue-ruled. Thin.
3. *Lrs. 1, 2.* Very similar to 1 in texture, but lighter in color, and laid. No printed head appears, but L. 2 (which is folded and measures 5.2 x 8.1) appears to be on a sheet that has been trimmed, while L. 1 is on a fragment of a larger sheet.
4. *Lrs. 3, 5.* Folded notepaper (5.3 x 8.3). Cream. Laid.
5. *Lrs. 4, 6.* Folded notepaper (4.8 x 7.5). Foreign make and watermark. L. 4 has been trimmed.
6. *Lrs. 7–12, 14–20, 25.* Folded notepaper (4.4 x 7). The first leaf is watermarked "Waterlows' / [design] / London"; the second, "Royal / English / Vellum."
7. *L. 13.* Half letterhead (Barr, Moering & Co., etc.). 10.3 x 8. Blue-ruled. Thin.
8. *Lrs. 21, 35.* Single, ruled sheet (8.4 x 10.6). Thin. Used chiefly by C. for his creative writing.
9. *Lrs. 22–24, 27, 28.* Folded notepaper (4.5 x 7.1). The first leaf is watermarked with an equestrian statue; the second, with "Jeanne D'Arc / Anno Domini / 1429."
10. *L. 26.* Single notehead (Barr, Moering & Co., etc.). 5.6 x 8.8. Faintly ruled. Thin.
11. *L. 29.* Half letterhead (Barr, Moering & Co., etc.). 8 x 7. Blue-ruled. (Form 42.)
12. *Lrs. 30–32, 98.* Folded notepaper (4.5 x 7.1). Watermarked "Hieratica, etc." Grey.
13. *L. 33.* Similar to 11, but longer. 8 x 10.2. (Form 43.)
14. *L. 34.* Folded notepaper (4.4 x 6.9). Slate. Laid. (Very similar to App. III, no. 2.)

15. *L. 36*. Folded notepaper (4.4 x 6.9). Watermarked with an anchor in an oval, etc.
16. *Lrs. 37–42, 74–78*. Folded notepaper (4.5 x 7). Grey. Laid. Thick.
17. *L. 43*. Folded notepaper (4.4 x 7). Foreign make and watermark.
18. *Lrs. 44–49, 54, 57, 59, 61–63, 79*. Folded notepaper (4.4 x 7). Watermarked "Original / Culter Mill."
19. *Lrs. 50–52*. Single sheet (8.4 x 10.6). Cross-ruled in blue. L. 52 is on a fragment of a larger sheet.
20. *L. 53*. Single letterhead (Barr, Moering & Co., etc.). 8 x 10.1. Faintly ruled and thin, as 10, but the printed head bears a different address.
21. *Lrs. 55, 56, 64, 67*. Folded notepaper (4.5 x 7.1). Calendered.
22. *L. 58*. Folded notehead (Elstree, Herts.). 4 x 5.9.
23. *L. 60*. A fragment, perhaps of 20, though there are no perceptible lines.
24. *Lrs. 65, 66*. Folded notepaper (4.5 x 7.1). Watermarked "Apirie & Sons / 1891."
25. *Lrs. 68–70, 72*. As 24, but with "1887" instead of "1891."
26. *L. 71*. Half letterhead (Champel-les-Bains près Genève, etc.). 8.5 x 6.5. Cross-ruled in blue.
27. *L. 73*. Single notehead (Barr, Moering & Co., etc.). 5.4 x 8.7. Faintly ruled and thin, as 10, but the printed head bears a different address.
28. *Lrs. 80, 81*. Folded notepaper (4.4 x 7). Watermarked "Ravensbourne / TB & Co. / London."
29. *L. 82*. Folded notepaper (4.5 x 7.1). Watermarked "Parchment, etc."
30. *L. 83*. Single notepaper (4.5 x 7). Chequered (invisible) and watermarked "Old / English / Chequer."
31. *Lrs. 84–89*. Folded notepaper (4.4 x 7). Bluish green.
32. *L. 89, n. 1 (to Buls)* ; *L. 92*. Folded notepaper (3.8 x 6). Watermarked "De La Rue & Co. / London."
33. *L. 90*. Folded notehead (Champel-les-Bains près Genève, etc.). 5.3 x 8.6. Ruled oblongs.
34. *L. 91*. Folded sheet (5.3 x 8.2). Quadrille.
35. *Lrs. 93–96*. Folded notehead (Pent Farm, etc.). 4.4 x 7.1.
36. *L. 97*. Folded notepaper (4.4 x 7). Watermarked "Bonny Brig / TB & Co. / London."
37. *L. 99*. Single letterhead (Pent Farm, etc.). 8 x 10. Watermarked "Original / Rockleigh / Mill."
38. *L. 100*. Folded notepaper (4.5 x 6). Lavender. Thin.

39. *Lrs. 101–103.* Single letterhead (Someries, Luton, Beds.). 7.9 x 9.7. Watermarked "Conqueror / London." Reinforced by gauze. Laid.
40. *L. 104.* Folded notepaper (5.1 x 6.9). Watermarked "Royal / English Linen / Air-Dried."
41. *L. 105.* Single, ruled sheet (8 x 9.7). Used chiefly by C. for his creative writing. (Cf. 8.)
42. *Lrs. 106–109.* Single letterhead (Capel House, etc.). 8 x 10. Blue. Stiff.
43. *L. 110.* Single letterhead (Oswalds, etc.). 7 x 9.

BIBLIOGRAPHY

Books, etc., referred to only once are not always included in this list, which contains, on the other hand, a few works not previously mentioned. For a key to special abbreviations, see p. xxv.

Almanach de Gotha; annuaire généalogique, diplomatique et statistique. . . . Gotha: J. Perthes (etc.).

Annuaire de la presse française et étrangère et du monde politique. Paris. 1880–.

Bibliographie de la France; journal général de l'imprimerie et de la librairie. Paris: Au cercle de la librairie. 1857–.

Bibliographie du Congo, 1880–1895, par A.-J. Wauters . . . avec la collaboration de M. Ad. Buyl. Bruxelles: Administration du mouvement géographique. 1895.

Biographie nationale . . . de Belgique, publiée par l'Académie royale. . . . T. 27. Bruxelles. 1866–1938.

The Bookman. New York. 1895–1933.

Brandes, Georg. Poland. New York. 1903.

Catalogue général des livres imprimés de la bibliothèque nationale. Paris. 1897–.

Charteris, Evan. The Life and Letters of Sir Edmund Gosse. London and New York. 1931.

Chodźko, A. B. Słownik polsko-angielski, i angielsko-polski. . . . Chicago, Ill.: Polish American Pub. Co. n.d.

Le Congo illustré. Voyages et travaux des Belges dans l'État indépendant du Congo. Publié sous la direction de A.-J. Wauters. T. 4. Bruxelles. 1892–95.

Conrad, Jessie. Joseph Conrad and His Circle. New York. 1935.

—— Joseph Conrad as I Knew Him. London. 1926.

Conrad, Joseph. Lettres françaises, avec une introduction et des notes de G. Jean-Aubry. Paris: Gallimard. [1930?] [*LF*]

—— Works. (Uniform Edition, London, and Concord Edition, Garden City, N.Y.). 1923–29. Of the cited component parts of different volumes, "Heart of Darkness" is in *Youth;* and "Geography and Some Explorers," "Ocean Travel," "The Congo Diary," and "The 'Torrens': A Personal Tribute" are in *Last Essays.*

Le Correspondant. Paris. 1855–1933.

CURLE, RICHARD. Conrad to a Friend: 150 Selected Letters from Joseph Conrad to Richard Curle, edited with an Introduction and Notes by R. C. New York. 1928.

Dictionnaire des écrivains belges. *See* Seyn, Eugène de.

Encyclopædia Britannica. 11th ed. Cambridge, England, and New York. 1910–11.

Figaro illustré. Paris: J. Boussod, Manzi, Joyant & Cie. 1883–.

Le Figaro ("Supplément littéraire"). Paris. 1875–.

FORD, FORD M. Return to Yesterday. New York. 1932.

FRY, E. A. Almanacks for Students of English History. London: Phillimore. 1915.

GALSWORTHY, JOHN. "Reminiscences of Conrad," in *Castles in Spain & Other Screeds*. London. 1927.

GARNETT, EDWARD. Letters from Joseph Conrad, 1895–1924. Edited with Introduction and Notes by Edward Garnett. Indianapolis. 1928.

GORDAN, JOHN D. Joseph Conrad: His Development as a Novelist from Amateur to Professional. (Harvard doctoral dissertation, 1939, now being published by the Harvard University Press with the title: *Joseph Conrad: The Making of a Novelist.*)

Ilustrowana encyklopedja Trzaski, Everta i Michalskiego. T. 5. Warsaw. [*c.* 1928.]

JEAN-AUBRY, G. Joseph Conrad in the Congo. London: "The Bookman's Journal" office. 1926.

——Joseph Conrad: Life & Letters. 2 vols. London and New York. 1927. [*LL*]

Journal de Bruxelles. *See* "Poradowski, A."

The Journal of Arnold Bennett. 3 vols. New York. 1932–33.

KEATING, GEORGE T. A Conrad Memorial Library, the Collection of George T. Keating. New York. 1929.

Larousse du XXe siècle. T. 6. Paris: Lib. Larousse. 1928–33.

The Library of John Quinn. Part I. New York: The Anderson Galleries. Sale No. 1768. 1923.

Lloyd's Register of British and Foreign Shipping. London: Wyman and Sons (etc.).

LORENTOWICZ, J., et CHMURSKI, A. M. La Pologne en France, essai d'une bibliographie raisonnée, I. (Institut d'études slaves de l'Université de Paris. Bibliothèque polonaise. IV.) Paris: Champion. 1935.

LUBBOCK, BASIL. The Colonial Clippers. Glasgow. 1921.

LÜTKEN, OTTO. "Joseph Conrad in the Congo," in the *London Mercury*, XXII, no. 127 (May, 1930), pp. 40–43. [*See also* no. 129, pp. 261–263, and no. 130, pp. 350 f.]

MARROT, H. V. The Life and Letters of John Galsworthy. London. 1936.

MORF, GUSTAV. The Polish Heritage of Joseph Conrad. London. [1929?]

Le Mouvement géographique; journal populaire des sciences géographiques. Publié sous la direction de A.-J. Wauters. Bruxelles: Administration du mouvement géographique. 1884–.

New English Dictionary on Historical Principles. Ed. by J. A. H. Murray. 13 vols. Oxford. 1888–1928. [*NED*]

Polski słownik biograficzny. Cracow. 1935–.

"Poradowski, A.," an obituary in the *Journal de Bruxelles* for 12 Feb., 1890.

Revue des Deux Mondes. Paris. 1829–. [*RDM*]

Revue encyclopédique; recueil documentaire universel et illustré, publié sous la direction de M. G. Moreau. Paris: Lib. Larousse. 1891–1900. (T. VI [1896], no. 169, p. 882, contains a brief article on Mme. P., together with the picture of her reproduced in this book.)

The Saturday Review of Literature. New York. 1924–.

SEYN, EUGÈNE DE. Dictionnaire des écrivains belges. T. 2. Bruges: Eds. "Excelsior." 1930–31.

Słownik angielsko-polski i polsko-angielski. Ed. by W. Kierst. T. 2. Warsaw: Trzaski, Everta i Michalskiego. 1926–28.

Le Temps. Paris.

TOMLINSON, H. M. Below London Bridge. London. 1934.

WHYTE, F. William Heinemann: A Memoir. New York. 1929.

WISE, THOMAS J. A Bibliography of the Writings of Joseph Conrad (1895–1921). 2d ed. London. 1921.

INDEX